ALL GOD'S
PEOPLE

ALL GOD'S PEOPLE

Effective Catechesis in a
Diverse Church

DONNA TOLIVER GRIMES

THE EFFECTIVE CATECHETICAL LEADER
Series Editor Joe Paprocki, DMin

LOYOLAPRESS.
A JESUIT MINISTRY
Chicago

LOYOLA PRESS.
A JESUIT MINISTRY

3441 N. Ashland Avenue
Chicago, Illinois 60657
(800) 621-1008
www.loyolapress.com

Unless otherwise indicated, Scripture quotations contained herein are from the *New Revised Standard Version Bible: Catholic Edition*, copyright © 1993 and 1989 by the Division of Christian Education of the National Council of the Churches of Christ in the U.S.A. Used by permission. All rights reserved.

Scripture quotations designated NABRE are from the *New American Bible* revised edition © 2008, 1991, 1986, 1970. Confraternity of Christian Doctrine, Inc., Washington DC. All Rights Reserved.

Cover art credit: iStock.com/lushik.

ISBN: 978-0-8294-4534-3
Library of Congress Control Number: 2017956881

Printed in the United States of America.
17 18 19 20 21 22 23 24 25 26 27 Versa 10 9 8 7 6 5 4 3 2 1

Contents

Welcome to The Effective Catechetical Leader Series

The Effective Catechetical Leader series provides skills, strategies, and approaches to ensure success for leaders of parish faith-formation programs. It will benefit anyone working with catechists, including Directors of Religious Education, pastors, diocesan directors, and catechetical training programs. Combining theory and practice, this series will

- provide practical instruction and printable resources;
- define the role of the catechetical leader and offer specific and practical strategies for leading, collaborating, and delegating;
- offer approaches for leading and catechizing in a more evangelizing way; and
- describe best practices for recruiting, training, and forming catechists; developing a vision for faith formation; forming an advisory board; planning and calendaring; networking with colleagues; selecting quality catechetical resources; handling the administrative aspects of the ministry; and identifying various groups to be catechized and approaches that meet the unique needs of those various groups.

Whether you are starting out as a catechetical leader or have been serving as one for many years, **The Effective Catechetical Leader** series will help you use every aspect of this ministry to proclaim the gospel and invite people to discipleship.

About This Book

Disciples of Christ come in all ages and colors, but they also come from different backgrounds and bring with them diverse gifts, needs, opportunities, and challenges. As a result, catechesis must never take the form of one-size-fits-all. While the gospel message is eternal, our messaging (how we share that timeless message) needs to adapt to an ever-changing reality or we risk being perceived as irrelevant. This sixth volume of **The Effective Catechetical Leader** takes a close look at the many groups of people to be catechized—from school-age children to young adults, from parents to the catechists themselves—and offers strategies and tips to effectively engage all of them in life-giving, gospel-centered faith formation.

1

Rights and Responsibilities
in Catechesis

Welcome to the Community

It's a joyful and familiar scene. The family gathers around the baptismal font for their child's baptism. Parents, grandparents, and godparents are beaming with pride. The child is wiggling and fussy. It all looks perfectly ordinary. Yet, during this ceremony, the ordinary elements of water, oil, a candle, a white garment all become sacred. Holy words of blessing are said in the name of the Father, Son, and Holy Spirit, and the community enters the mystery of initiation with the candidate.

In the celebration of baptism, the principal roles—priest, godparents, or sponsors—are pretty clear. But the role of the onlookers in the congregation may not be so clearly understood. For many people in the community witnessing this blessed event, a question may linger in the back of their minds: *And now, who is responsible for instructing and forming this new disciple?*

How Do Disciples Form Disciples?

Actually, the entire Church bears the duty and responsibility for raising up disciples. Jesus addressed this in his commission to his disciples after his Resurrection: "Go therefore and *make disciples* of all nations, *baptizing* them in the name of the Father and of the Son and of the Holy Spirit, and *teaching* them to obey everything that I have commanded you" (Matt. 28:19–20, emphasis added).

By virtue of baptism, all disciples of Jesus Christ (i.e., Christians) receive this charge to make more disciples, baptizing and teaching them all that the Savior commanded. So how do we, as disciples, form more disciples? The most direct and purposeful way is to invite our family members—spouses and children—to become disciples of Christ. Then, often indirectly, our Christian witness touches the lives of those around us: friends, neighbors, associates, and other individuals in our community and workplace, who are drawn to Christ by our example. But discipleship doesn't just happen all at once!

In his book *Will There Be Faith? A New Vision for Educating and Growing Disciples* (HarperCollins, 2011), Thomas Groome emphasizes that people seeking to know God are co-responsible in this spiritual journey. They have the capacity or "response-ability" to accept God's invitation to draw nearer. Groome synthesizes the new understanding of the role of the laity articulated in the documents of the Second Vatican Council: "The Council's statements are a clarion call to a new level of co-responsibility for our faith and Church. Rather than being divided into providers and dependents, teachers and taught, baptism unites and calls everyone to lifelong growth into holiness of life . . . in carrying on Jesus' mission and ministry to the world" (78). Catechetical leaders would do well to remind parents and sponsors that "baptism is an act of faith, not of magic. Christians don't grow into . . . holiness of life and co-responsibility for the Church's mission just by being baptized" (78). As I said, discipleship doesn't just happen all at once!

Passing It On

Christians accept the baton of faith much like runners in a 4 x 400-meter relay race: it is passed from one to another. Sometimes, because of a weak grip, they drop the baton of faith somewhere on the track. When that happens, some runners will stop to retrieve the baton; others will continue running their leg of the race, drawn to the goal yet unaware that they have nothing to hand to the next runner. Also, there are those who will attempt to pass the baton to the next runner without ensuring that the teammate has a firm grip on it. Fortunately, some relay runners grasp the baton and run straight ahead, releasing it only when the next runner grasps the baton of faith securely.

Christians generally grasp Jesus' command to baptize. In addition, many Christians make it their business to teach the faith to their children and grandchildren. Any efforts to make new disciples beyond the family circle are usually more casual, happening almost accidentally when faith and good works are observed by friends, neighbors, coworkers, and associates over time. Often, these very Christians who attend to the spiritual formation of their own kin do not firmly grasp Jesus' command to *make disciples of all*.

Providing faith formation for one's children is not simply a nice thing to do for them; it is their canonical right to receive effective catechetical instruction. We are told in the *Code of Canon Law* that the Church has "a proper and grave duty to take care of the catechesis of the Christian people" (#773). This responsibility flows from the bishop as principal catechist in the diocese to the pastor and catechetical leaders. These teachers of the faith may be assisted by families, Catholic schools, religious associations, diocesan offices, and various ministries of the parish, among others. God acts simultaneously in the hearts of individuals and within the heart of the community, ensuring that those who respond to the invitation to follow Jesus may have full access to his saving vision.

The Scope of Jesus' Vision

What might it have been like to follow Jesus in his daily life and see what he saw? Let's think about this and really try to imagine it. When Jesus was going to the Temple or seeing friends or doing his work, whom did he pass along the way? Undoubtedly there were women and girls carrying large jugs of water and gathering food for the family meal. He saw laborers and merchants, and farmers directing dusty oxen, goats, and sheep.

Walking into the public spaces of the towns around, Jesus likely observed parents and grandparents fully engaged in their daily chores, surrounded by children playfully tagging one another, as well as poor beggars on the road seeking food and encouragement. Certainly he came across childless adults, shamed in a society where offspring signified God's favor. The Master passed individuals with seeping wounds, damaged limbs, and birth defects. He shared the roads with rich and poor, proud and humble, strong and weak. Jesus must have acknowledged the many people he encountered, including many with limited vision and missing teeth. There were the beautiful and privileged, and there were those wearing the only cloak they owned.

Sacred Scripture indicates that Jesus observed the natural world of plants and animals as well as humanity. Each day our Lord, fully human and fully divine, was confronted with an array of smells—both pleasant and repugnant. He must have overheard angry disputes and witnessed abuses of power. Jesus absorbed myriad human experiences, which he brought to his Father in prayer. The Father responded with the wisdom and understanding evident in Jesus' teaching and miracles.

As word of Jesus' compassion blazed through the region, people were drawn to his acts of kindness and respect, his poignant explanations too numerous to capture fully in the oral and written accounts of his life and ministry on earth. Many were attracted by his powerful works and authoritative teaching. They yearned to hear him, to touch the hem of his garment, to stand in his shadow, to catch a glimpse of the young rabbi from Nazareth. There is a contemporary gospel song that expresses this desire of those who heard about Jesus: "While you're blessing others, do not pass me by."

Likewise, when Jesus spoke to the multitudes, imagine what his audiences looked like. Read Matt. 5:1–12. Close your eyes for a few minutes. Visualize Jesus, surrounded by the crowd listening to what we refer to today as the Sermon on the Mount. Do you see women present as well as men? Are there adolescents and seniors in the crowd? Looking out, can you see parents nudging youth to pay attention or coaxing little ones to sleep contentedly while Mother listens to this exciting message? Isn't it likely that some people physically struggled to hear Jesus' words? That others enjoyed his calming presence although they were intellectually challenged to understand his message? How did folks in the crowd manage to sit comfortably on the hard surfaces amid sticks and stones?

Jesus taught whoever came and spoke to them in ways they could grasp and relate to. He scanned the crowds in front of him as well as people around the periphery. He even caught people spying from the branches of a sycamore tree, as Zacchaeus did. Jesus' vision was clear and all-encompassing.

A Wide-Angle Lens

When you consider the people in your care who need to be catechized, does your view span the full horizon of the community before you, or is your sight locked straight ahead? When it comes to effective catechetical leadership, we need to have a wide vision, as Jesus did. In too many parishes there is a tilt toward catechesis for school-age children, and it is particularly skewed toward sacrament preparation. Often success is measured by the number of first-time communicants, confirmands, and catechumens who pass through our church doors each year. Yet, this unbalanced approach does not serve us well when it consumes more than its fair share of catechetical resources—personnel, materials, time, budget, and enthusiasm—and leads to neglecting or underserving the faith-formation needs of other groups in the parish.

Take a good look at the parish or faith community for which you serve as a catechetical leader. Prayerfully listen to what the Holy Spirit reveals to you about the formation needs of this parish or faith community. Consider the full range of parishioners. Every one of them has a right to effective catechetical instruction, and the Church has a duty to provide it. This explains why you have the position of catechetical leader. The full range of parishioners includes not only those who eagerly attend and participate in Mass each Sunday but also those who attend weekly Mass sporadically and those who sit passively in the pews. Pray about the formation needs of those appearing distracted or disengaged. Include in your reflections and prayerful consideration those who are already actively engaged in liturgy and outreach.

One way to view the situation with fresh eyes and a wide-angle lens is to attend each of the weekend Masses more than once throughout the year. Take the time to scan the congregation and to talk with some of the people who attend those Masses that you typically do not attend. If you habitually attend the early Sunday Mass, make it a point to go to the late Sunday and Saturday vigil Masses. Similarly, if Mass in the parish, in the diocese, or on campus is celebrated in other languages or liturgical styles than your norm, attend those as well. Much like the experience of a regular driver riding public transportation for a change, you will discover other segments of the community and develop new perspectives and approaches for catechetical ministry.

Assessing Catechetical Vision: Fusion of Rights and Responsibilities

As already noted, every baptized individual has a right to effective catechetical instruction, and the Church has a duty and obligation to provide such faith formation. The *Catechism of the Catholic Church* provides some insights concerning the duties of those to be catechized. It begins at the source: "The desire for God is written on the human heart, because man is created by God and for God; and God never ceases to draw man to himself. Only in God will he find the truth and happiness he never stops searching for" (*CCC*, #27).

Catholic teaching further recognizes that "faith is a gift of God, a supernatural virtue infused by him. Before this faith can be exercised, man must have the grace of God to move and assist him; he must have the interior helps of the Holy Spirit, who moves the heart and converts it to God, who opens the eyes of the mind and 'makes it easy for all to accept and believe the truth'" (*CCC*, #153). Those who have received the Holy Spirit in baptism also receive the grace and free will to seek knowledge of God.

Moreover, to the best of their ability, disciples of Christ have a lifelong responsibility to form a moral conscience, to follow the example of Christ, and to choose good over evil. As the *National Directory for Catechesis* states, "While moral conscience reflects God's law written in the human heart, it needs to be formed and informed. The judgments it renders must be enlightened" (*NDC*, #42C). Likewise, the one being catechized "must be an active subject, conscious and co-responsible, and not merely a silent and passive recipient" (*GDC*, #167).

Thus, the catechetical task is truly a collaboration between those who desire to know God and those who are directing them to the One they seek. Ideally, both are being formed, informed, and transformed. One may be a catechist and the other an apprentice, but they are both teaching and learning together. As the *Catechism* indicates,

"[T]his search for God *demands of man every effort* of intellect, a sound will, 'an upright heart,' *as well as the witness of others who teach him* to seek God" (*CCC*, #30, emphasis added).

The Role of Evangelization

The New Evangelization addresses not only those who know God but also those who never knew God and those who did at one time. This fresh teaching on evangelization speaks of rekindling the fire of faith that once burned in people's hearts but may have dimmed. Evangelizing in the Catholic tradition is not about knocking on the doors of neighbors or leaving tracts in coffee shops and bus terminals. It is, however, something we are all called to participate in. We do this in community, in obedience to promptings of the Holy Spirit, and in fulfillment of the Great Commission of Christ to "make disciples of all nations."

Therefore, effective catechesis is continuous formation throughout the life of a disciple—all disciples. There is neither pill nor formula that will make the process happen quickly and smoothly. We need God's ongoing pruning. We need God's touch on our hearts and minds throughout the ebbs and flows of spiritual development, through all the seasons of a lifelong, continuous encounter with our Maker. The human attention span can be short. We tune in and we tune out. Yet, even when the presence of God is not at the surface of our consciousness, God is still with us. We desperately need the Spirit of God, whether we realize it or not. Ongoing faith formation for all of God's people ensures that God's saving presence will not be taken for granted or forgotten.

Faith Formation for *Everyone*?

The notion of catechizing *all* God's people can be overwhelming! Given human limitations and finite resources, there is so much to know, to teach, to learn in the time allocated to religious education. Dioceses establish guidelines and mandate assessments. Often, our religious-formation structures and processes tend to mirror the school model, with nine- to ten-month terms, age-based classes, weekly assignments, periodic testing, and proficiency standards. Given all those complexities, how can a catechetical leader possibly target other groups for faith formation? What are reasonable expectations for catechetical leaders? Where do we focus attention, and how do we measure success?

Begin with the understanding that the object of catechetical instruction is not simply the transmission of Church doctrine, Catholic prayers, the Bible, or the sacraments. The heart and soul of catechesis is a person: Jesus Christ. As the *National Directory for Catechesis* elaborates,

> The object of catechesis is communion with Jesus Christ. Catechesis leads people to enter the mystery of Christ, to encounter him, and to discover themselves and the meaning of their lives in him. . . . Christ is the living center of catechesis, who draws all persons to his Father through the Holy Spirit. . . . The definitive aim of catechesis is "to put people not only in touch but in communion, in intimacy, with Jesus Christ: only he can lead us to the love of the Father in the Spirit and make us share in the life of the Holy Trinity." (*NDC*, #19B)

I confess that I didn't know this as a young catechist. Nor did I operate with such clear vision as a parish Director of Religious Education. Rather, I was more like sister Martha, "worried and distracted by many things" (Luke 10:41). I now know that our perspective can be calibrated. God can and will adjust our attitudes if we open ourselves to his scrutiny. Pope Francis articulated beautifully what it means for us to be missionary disciples:

Pastoral ministry in a missionary style is not obsessed with the disjointed transmission of a multitude of doctrines to be insistently imposed. . . . [T]he message has to concentrate on the essentials, on what is most beautiful, most grand, most appealing and at the same time most necessary. The message is simplified, while losing none of its depth and truth, and thus becomes all the more forceful and convincing. (*Evangelii Gaudium, The Joy of the Gospel,* #35)

We have begun this book about discipling all God's people by identifying their rights and our responsibilities in catechesis. Now we turn to the catechetical needs of distinct groups and effective approaches for reaching them.

Summary: Searching for the Treasure

The kingdom of heaven is like treasure hidden in a field, which someone found and hid; then in his joy he goes and sells all that he has and buys that field. Again, the kingdom of heaven is like a merchant in search of fine pearls. On finding one pearl of great value, he went and sold all that he had and bought it. (Matt. 13:44–46)

In every age and in every corner of the world, people search for the treasure that God has planted deep in the heart of humankind. As a catechetical leader, your role is to assist people in uncovering this true treasure planted deep within the human heart. This requires not only knowledge, skills, and a positive attitude but also a vision for catechesis that includes everyone—people of all ages, ethnicities, socioeconomic levels, and abilities. As you set out to focus on the people to be catechized in your pastoral setting, ask yourself the following questions. Do you

- see them?
- hear what they say and don't say?
- know them?

- hope for them?
- receive and learn from them?
- pray for and pray with them?
- respect them?
- see Jesus Christ in them?
- recognize them as brothers and sisters?
- love them?

For Reflection and Discussion

- Are the catechetical efforts and resources in your parish/faith community distributed equitably among the faithful?
- For which demographic(s) is the catechetical program thriving (e.g., children, RCIA, young adults, seniors)? Who is underserved?
- To create a more comprehensive outreach to various groups in the parish when it comes to faith formation, what do you need to do?

Growing as a Catechetical Leader

As a citizen of the United States, you have certain rights and responsibilities. Think about and identify those rights that you feel most strongly about and would even fight for. Now think about the fact that all the baptized people in your parish have a right to high-quality catechetical instruction. Imagine if a new ruling power restricted or even denied that right. How might that scenario change the way you approach providing faith formation for those in your parish?

Go to www.loyolapress.com/ECL to access the worksheet.

Suggested Action

When we take photographs, some people may be cropped out inadvertently. If you were to snap a photograph of the people involved in your parish's faith-formation efforts, whom would you identify as being "cropped out"? In the days ahead, make a list of these groups, and begin praying for the grace needed to address their faith-formation needs.

For Further Consideration

The Code of Canon Law (Rome: Libreria Editrice Vaticana, 1983).

General Directory for Catechesis (Washington, DC: United States Conference of Catholic Bishops, 1998).

National Directory for Catechesis (Washington, DC: United States Conference of Catholic Bishops, 2005).

Will There Be Faith? A New Vision for Educating and Growing Disciples. Thomas H. Groome (New York: HarperCollins, 2011).

2

Goodbye, Catholic Bubble: Diversity, Mobility, and Various Isms in Today's Culture

Catholics Banded Together

Since our country's founding, the religious culture of the United States has always been distinctly Protestant. The prejudice that Catholics weathered as the country became a union of states required that Catholics band together for survival. Anti-Catholic rhetoric was painful but fortified the Catholic faithful as fire tests gold. The election of John Fitzgerald Kennedy as the first Catholic president in 1960 was as momentous as the election of Barack Hussein Obama, the first African American president nearly half a century later. The election of the first woman president someday will rock our world as well.

Today it may be difficult to imagine a time when Catholics banded together simply to provide for the most basic needs of their families—food, shelter, and employment. Historically, exclusion from the mainstream of American institutions required this religious minority to draw on their faith and on the power of their group as a way of life. Out of necessity, a strong Catholic identity emerged.

As with other European immigrants and Christian denominations, bonds of friendship and fellowship were promoted (among Catholics) through various fraternal societies, guilds, and clubs, as Sherry Weddell notes in her book *Forming Intentional Disciples*. Naturally, marriages and business alliances formed as well. Within this familiar climate, favors were bestowed, recommendations were provided, introductions were made, and social support networks took shape.

Initially, Catholics responded to signs that read No Irish Need Apply and more subtle forms of employment discrimination by hiring their own. They gained economic strength through the creation of labor guilds. They formed volunteer fire and safety patrols that grew into municipal fire and police departments, providing stable, respectable jobs that passed through generations. Like other ethnic minorities, Catholics cared for their sick, orphans, and elderly. They pooled hard-earned nickels and dimes to ensure that loved ones received a proper burial at the end of life.

Thus, Catholics established schools, hospitals, social-service agencies, benevolent societies, and networks. Catholic immigrants from Europe brought over or sent for their clergy and religious orders to help them sustain the faith in this new land. These institutions contributed in numerous ways to the transmission of Catholic faith. A crucifix on the wall of every hospital room, the habits worn by those who staffed Catholic service agencies, and the visible presence of Catholic fraternal organizations at public events all signaled a growing and influential Catholic presence. Motivated by their faith, individuals and Catholic organizations generously and significantly contributed to the prosperity of this nation.

The fruit of this missionary activity includes Catholic institutions that extend compassion, support, and the Catholic brand well beyond the Catholic circle. If you were to name the institutions that are big players in your area, no doubt a Catholic hospital, university or high school, social-service agency, or nonprofit association would be among them. Another way to ponder this is to imagine how different this country might be if all the practicing Catholics vanished.

At the same time that the Catholic star was rising institutionally, the social status of Catholics elevated the group economically. According to Pew Research (2014 U.S. Religious Landscape Study), roughly one in five Catholics are in the top income bracket, which is the same as the nation as a whole, meaning that Catholics in general have "arrived" economically. The Catholic expression of Christianity is the largest single religious denomination in the United States today. At any academic level, a Catholic education carries the brand of high quality. A large segment of CEOs, corporate leaders, and professionals in the United States are (or were) Catholic. As of the writing of this book, Catholics hold the majority of seats on the U.S. Supreme Court and compose one-third of the members of Congress.

Unity of Faith Preserved in Many Flavors

As waves of immigrants arrived here from different parts of Europe in the early nineteenth century, Catholics organized themselves by language and country of origin. It is not surprising, then, how a national parish model took root and flourished here well into the twentieth century. In large urban centers, particularly in the East and Midwest—Boston, New York, Philadelphia, Pittsburgh, Milwaukee, Cincinnati, St. Louis, and Chicago, for example—Irish, German, Italian, Lithuanian, and Polish parishes were situated within close walking distance of one another. Each professed the same creed, and the liturgical rites remained intact. Before the Second Vatican Council, worship in Latin united Catholics everywhere. Meanwhile, selected feast days and related rituals and prayers that were practiced in particular communities transmitted the imprint of culture along with the articles of faith.

In the Catholic world, through the middle of the twentieth century, folks remained loosely united as a universal church. Silently making the sign of the cross shouted, "Catholic over here!" Catholics were taught that ours was the "One True Faith." Some may remember when, prior to the Second Vatican Council, Catholics were forbidden to enter other churches. Mixed marriages, though permitted, were discouraged. To be married in the Catholic Church—joined in the sacrament of matrimony—meant that the non-Catholic spouse had certified in writing that any resulting children would be raised Catholic. Forces within the Church, the family, the neighborhood, and society-at-large sustained what we can call the "Catholic bubble"—a homogenous, insular context in which the Catholic faith was able to soak into the marrow of individuals without interference from out-side factors. It was as if individuals were marinated in Catholicism. As a result, all that was needed in the area of faith formation was the grasping of doctrinal concepts, which were delivered through the question-and-answer format of the *Baltimore Catechism*.

Another phenomenon of ethnic parishes emerged as a consequence of segregation laws and racial isolation practices around the country that affected all regions, not only the South. As a result, African Americans, Asian Americans, Native Americans, Hispanic Americans, and new groups of immigrants created their own Catholic enclaves.

Some ethnic communities received pastoral support from designated religious orders that exercised a missionary vocation. The Josephite priests (Mill Hill Fathers), Spiritans (Holy Ghost Fathers), and Sisters of the Blessed Sacrament are three examples of missionary religious communities dedicated to ministry for Black Catholics. In a similar way, the Claretians and Dominicans (to name a few) have been at the forefront of ministry in the Latino community, while the Passionists and Redemptorists are among several religious communities who have been prominent in ministering in the Asian community.

Still, other groups of people received scant pastoral care, if any. In some cases, they were ecstatic to have access to a priest or other pastoral minister who spoke their native language of Kreyol, Bhutan, or Lakota. Yet, they persisted in their practice of the faith. These Catholics, who settled here from lands other than Europe or were present when others arrived, practiced the faith through their own cultural lenses when possible. They honored certain saints, contextualized sacred spaces with their own music, customs, gestures, and aesthetics. Essentially, they translated the Good News into their mother tongue.

While we may not always be conscious of its influence, culture plays a defining role in our lives and in our Catholic faith today. Just as we don't usually think about each breath we take, how it flows through our body and makes possible our actions and thoughts, so culture is the powerful silent partner in the navigation system of our lives. Culture is vital to understanding ourselves and making sense of the world.

Movement to Shared Parishes

The national/ethnic parish model achieved a measure of success while the groups remained separated, but this order has become unsustainable given current demographic and social changes in American society. One of those changes is the increased mobility that accompanied infrastructure and technological advances. Creation of the interstate highway system during the 1950s, followed by greater access to auto, rail, and air travel for business and personal destinations really got Americans traveling farther and more frequently. In addition to short-term travel, military service, education, and career opportunities increased options for longer stints away from home and even relocation.

The period after WWI through the late 1960s saw a major migration of African Americans from the South to the North and West. A generation later, European American WWII veterans used GI benefits to purchase homes in new communities emerging beyond city borders. Fast forward to the present; the trend toward more mobility has impacted decisions about where to attend church and how often.

Demographic changes, increased mobility, reduced Mass attendance, and economic fluctuations are some of the critical factors that
have led bishops to make the difficult decision to merge and close
parishes in recent years, particularly in urban areas and their close
suburbs, and especially in the Northeast and Midwest. Even when
parishes seem to be on life support, mergers and closings are emotionally painful to pastors and parishioners. You may recall news stories
about parishioners camped out in their churches to protest such closings. Less publicized are the desperate campaigns to bring about a
change of course. Undoubtedly, the newly constituted parish will face
cultural challenges. Hard lessons have uncovered approaches to miti-
gate the damage. The United States Conference of Catholic Bishops
(USCCB) includes on their Web site (www.usccb.org) an excellent
series of videos that illustrate the cultural diversity of the Church today
in the United States.

Like many other denominations, the Catholic Church is trending
toward multicultural, or shared, parishes. At this time, 38 percent of
Catholic parishes celebrate Mass in at least one language other than
English. And the number is increasing, especially in the South and
West, where the Church is growing. In the transition, pastors, parish
leaders, and people in the pews are challenged to quickly modify their
view of community.

Multicultural parishes appeal to a broad group of Catholics but,
unfortunately, not to everyone. Shared parishes tend to attract younger
Catholics, families with small children, and individuals who have trav-
eled extensively for education, work, or pleasure. Increasingly, the
determinants in parish selection are not geography but homiletic deliv-
ery, musical style, sense of community, and Mass-time options. More
often than not, the faithful no longer walk to church with family and
friends. Instead, they drive to the parish of their choice, with at least
one-fifth of them passing several other Catholic churches along the

way. A reconfiguration of parishes naturally affects the local system and design of parish-based religious-formation programs.

Unlocking the Locks

Imagine catechesis as a ministry of opening locked doors for the multitude waiting to enter heaven. The pastor hands you a set of keys. Which is the right one for the faithful remnant families who have been in the parish for generations? Is it the same key that will get Mrs. Jones to commit to bringing her children to religious-education consistently each week? Did you know that she is raising them alone following the divorce a year ago? Since Dad is out of the house now, will he bring the children to religious-education class, or will he take them to breakfast and the park on his custodial weekends?

There is no typical American family these days. The television series *The Waltons* depicted a slice of life during the Great Depression of the 1930s. The Cleavers (*Leave It to Beaver*) projected an airbrushed image of America's budding white suburban family of the late 1950s. In the 1970s, *The Brady Bunch* depicted the reality of a blended family, although it continued to present the typical American family as suburban, white, upper-middle class. Around the same time, however, Diahann Carroll's breakthrough show *Julia* depicted a single Black mom raising her son—a show that critics claimed was "unrealistic."

Families today comprise fewer married mothers and fathers raising their biological offspring or adoptees. What our culture now recognizes as "family" may include single parents, grandparents caring for grandchildren, same-sex couples raising children, adults cohabiting with or without children, blended families following the death of a spouse or divorce, and still other familial arrangements.

While there was a time when Catholics married only Catholics, today that is no longer true. As a result, Catholics can be found under the same roof with Christians of other denominations, non-Christians, agnostics, and even atheists. According to the Center for Applied Research in the Apostolate (CARA) research, fewer than one in three U.S. Catholics consider it "very important" to marry another Catholic (CARA, 2007). For today's catechetical leader, the realities of ecumenism and interreligious dialogue are no longer peripheral issues but are of heightened importance.

Impact of Individualism and Materialism on the Human Soul

Modern American culture presents specific challenges for catechesis and for enthusiastically embracing gospel values. For example, we value freedom in a sense that prioritizes the needs and desires of the individual over the community. We value pragmatism: "This practical orientation makes U.S. culture open to a wide variety of new ideas and possibilities but susceptible to utilitarian purposes" (*NDC* #10.E).

We are living in a place and time when much of what we use every day is disposable. There are extra packaging, seasonal clothing, and sleek kitchen gadgets that we must have. Our closets, garages, and storage units are stuffed with items we use only occasionally. How many souvenir ball caps and tote bags do you own? The expensive technology we need to work "smarter" is surpassed by newer, shinier items in less than two years. Although some forces are pushing back on extreme consumerism, it is truly a David-and-Goliath battle.

Pope Francis has repeatedly emphasized the perilous spiritual ramifications of acquiring so much stuff. One of those hazards is treating *people* as disposable. This happens on the interpersonal level. It is a by-product of a wealthy industrialized lifestyle in the United States. We see this manifested in the millions of God's children who are incarcerated, serving lengthy sentences under harsh conditions, and many for nonviolent crimes or while awaiting judgment. They are locked up out of sight and forgotten. As we hurry to our important destinations, we find ourselves stepping over and passing vulnerable people on the street. Whole classes of people are virtually regarded as expendables, as less than human. But the Good News is intended equally for the advantaged and disadvantaged. Our Church urges us, as Jesus did, to encounter one another with love, to be merciful, and to extend to others what God has so graciously gifted us.

Our contemporary social structure erects huge barriers to spiritual formation—specifically, the props of media and technology on which we rely. These are helpful to a point, but they can constrict the flow of loving exchange with God and neighbor. To those who don't know better, media's thin promises of untold pleasure, well-earned accolades, eternal health and beauty, and lasting security are more attractive than the Gospel's invitation to virtuous living. It is imperative that we as catechetical leaders realize that this is a spiritual life-or-death struggle.

Pope Francis pinpoints the challenge this way:

> [W]hen media and the digital world become omnipresent, their influence can stop people from learning how to live wisely, to think deeply and to love generously. . . . Real relationships with others, with all the challenges they entail, now tend to be replaced by a type of internet communication which enables us to choose or eliminate relationships at whim, thus giving rise to a new type of contrived emotion which has more to do with devices and displays than with other people and with nature. Today's media do enable us to communicate and to share our knowledge and affections. Yet at times they also shield us from direct contact with the pain, the fears and the joys of others and the complexity of their personal experiences. (*Laudato Si'*, #47)

These thoughts of Pope Francis compel us, as catechetical leaders, to face some very important issues: in a media-driven, technology-enhanced world, we must use those tools to open channels of authentic communication with God and with one another, and we must harness media and technology to illuminate the content of religious formation.

Still, there is no substitute for helping those we catechize to appreciate the natural world as a channel of communication with God. Sometimes, we all need to unplug, open a window, and enjoy the wonderful world with which God gifted us. Elsewhere, Pope Francis addresses how a relationship with the natural world helps us develop spiritually:

> Our insistence that each human being is an image of God should not make us overlook the fact that each creature has its own purpose. None is superfluous. The entire material universe speaks of God's love, his boundless affection for us. Soil, water, mountains: everything is, as it were, a caress of God. The history of our friendship with God is always linked to particular places which take on an intensely personal meaning; we all remember places, and revisiting those memories does us much good. Anyone who has grown up in the hills or used to sit by the spring to drink, or played outdoors in the neighborhood square; going back to these places is a chance to recover something of their true selves. (*Laudato Si'*, #84)

Embracing New Realities

It is more and more apparent to us that the traditional religious-education model has played out and is no longer as effective as it once was. Traditionally, religious-education programs were built on a school model. Catechists (teachers) relied primarily on textbooks, and students sat at desks or tables for an hour each week over the course of an academic calendar (September through May). They took a break in the summer and matriculated to the next grade in autumn. Diocesan standards established proficiencies and mandated testing. For many children, enduring another academic experience was the last thing they wanted to do.

Adult formation programs followed a similar pattern, despite mounds of research on adult learning styles and effective instruction methods. So, what truly motivates adults to invest in their own continued spiritual formation? Is it the prospect of sitting in a classroom for two hours on a weeknight?

As catechetical leaders, we are called to look past a pedagogy that relies solely on the imparting and ingesting of doctrinal knowledge as a means to spiritual nourishment. The traditional catechetical model assumed that the imparting of knowledge would lead to preferred behaviors, e.g., regular Mass attendance, receiving the sacraments, etc. We have since come to understand that belief follows active participation in community life and periods of inquiry, supported by information about the faith.

The goals of faith formation, according to Sherry Weddell, author of *Forming Intentional Disciples*, are transformation and life change. Weddell explains that "[t]o know in biblical terms means we really experience something in our hearts as well as our heads . . . [I]t is knowledge that leads to love, while love, in turn, makes us want to love more." Recognizing the divinity within those we strive to catechize is a first step to encountering people where they are. It will help us select the key that God is handing us to open their hearts to new life in Christ. Effective catechetical leaders cut through the noise of the world with this important message: "Jesus Christ is the human face of God and the divine face of humanity" (*NDC*, #21A).

With the weakening of family ties, increased mobility, and intense demands of work, study, and everyday living, people crave community. The Church offers that possibility, because communal life is at the heart of our Catholic identity. The new realities we face will challenge us, as catechetical leaders, to embrace new thinking with humility, commitment, patience, and clear focus.

Summary: Different Gifts, Same Spirit

There are different kinds of spiritual gifts but the same Spirit; there are different forms of service but the same Lord; there are different workings but the same God who produces all of them in everyone. To each individual the manifestation of the Spirit is given for some benefit. . . . But one and the same Spirit produces all of these, distributing them individually to each person as he wishes. (1 Cor. 12:4–7, 11, NABRE)

In a bygone era, many Catholics lived in insular Catholic communities where every aspect of life was seemingly connected to the Catholic faith and the local parish was the center of people's lives. This reality can be thought of as a "Catholic bubble." As a result of this insular nature, individuals were formed in the Catholic faith by the family and the community and needed only to receive "instruction" on the catechism to complete their formation.

Today, this "bubble" no longer exists as Catholics find themselves living in a culture that is characterized by diversity, mobility, pluralism, multiculturalism, secularism, relativism, and materialism. All these factors have radically changed the way people live and are formed, and they have implications for how the Church's catechetical efforts must continue to change to meet these ever-growing challenges. As a catechetical leader, you are called to recognize not only the complexity and diversity of the community you serve but also the unifying power of the Holy Spirit, who directs those gifts to be placed in the service of God's people.

For Reflection and Discussion

- What was the heritage of the founding members of your parish or of a parish you belonged to in the past? Which special saint from their heritage was honored in that parish?

- Given the fact that Catholics no longer tend to live in "Catholic bubbles" but now live in a pluralistic and secular society, what implications do you see for your catechetical ministry?
- What new approaches to faith formation do you think are necessary to combat the many cultural forces working against a spiritual life of discipleship?

Growing as a Catechetical Leader

A new evangelization is synonymous with mission, requiring the capacity to set out anew, go beyond boundaries, and broaden horizons. The new evangelization is the opposite of self-sufficiency, a withdrawal into oneself, a status quo mentality, and an idea that pastoral programs are simply to proceed as they did in the past. Today, a "business as usual" attitude can no longer be the case. Some local  Churches, already engaged in renewal, reconfirm the fact that now is the time for the Church to call upon every Christian community to evaluate their pastoral practice on the basis of the missionary character of their programs and activities (Synod of Bishops XIII, Ordinary General Assembly, *The New Evangelization for the Transmission of the Christian Faith*, Lineamenta, #10).

One of the pitfalls that catechetical leaders strive to avoid is the "business as usual" mentality. What aspects of your ministry do you think need revamping and renewal?

Go to www.loyolapress.com/ECL to access the worksheet.

Suggested Action

In the story of Jesus healing a man with a withered hand (Mark 3:1–6 and Matt. 12:9–14), Jesus demonstrates that compassion is at the heart of the law and that pastoral response is guided by concern for the other, not by self-interest. As catechetical leaders, we are compelled to ask ourselves if self-interest and pride are what motivate and drive us in our ministry. This tough question deserves an honest answer, and so do the faithful people we serve. It is easy to feel frustrated about sustaining a catechetical program that doesn't bring in the numbers of participants we hope it will attract. Yet, can we say with confidence that our appeal reaches folks where they are today?

Take some time to reflect on your ministry. Ask for the grace to be driven by compassion and concern for others, and grace to avoid the temptation to be motivated by self-interest.

For Further Consideration

America's Changing Religious Landscape (Washington, DC: Pew Research Center, May 12, 2015).

The Changing Face of Church: Shaping Catholic Parishes. David A. Ramey and Marti R. Jewell, DMin (Chicago: Loyola Press, 2010).

The Changing Face of U.S. Catholic Parishes. Mark M. Gray, Mary L. Gautier, and Melissa A. Cidade (Washington, DC: National Association for Lay Ministry, 2011).

National Directory for Catechesis (Washington, DC: United States Conference of Catholic Bishops, 2005).

3

The Word Became Flesh: Catechesis and Inculturation

Culture Is the Air We Breathe

Jesus was God Incarnate, the Word made flesh: fully divine and fully human. But, like all children around the world since the beginning of time, Jesus was *enculturated* (a sociological term) through daily interactions with his family and community. We must remember that Jesus' first utterance was not, "Did you not know that I must be in my Father's house?" (Luke 2:49). Rather, from the time of his infancy Jesus grew physically and intellectually and learned the language, customs, and taboos of his people. He absorbed their values, preferences, and moral codes. While eating meals, working with Joseph at the carpentry trade, and studying with other boys his age, Jesus observed Jewish law, celebrated religious feasts, and participated in worship. Consequently, he experienced friendship, pain, hunger, fatigue, and disappointment, like the rest of humanity.

We know from Gospel passages that Jesus joked with others, such as when he nicknamed the sons of Zebedee, James and John, the "Sons of Thunder" (Mark 3:17), something people of that era probably found funny. Being a gifted storyteller, Jesus must have enjoyed hearing good stories. It is also evident that Jesus prayerfully studied the Torah and that he more than casually observed people and life around him. His parables and analogies, his use of exaggeration and surprising reversals, all resonated with the daily experiences of his audiences. Jesus connected deeply with people through shared culture.

Culture Is Like an Iceberg

The term *culture* may be defined in a variety of ways. Persons from a prevailing (or majority) culture may have difficulty identifying features of their own culture and may not grasp the active influence of culture on their lives. On the other hand, persons living in a prevailing culture that is different from their own tend to be more aware of the characteristics in their own culture and in the prevailing culture. Recognizable differences in customs, behavior, and language (deeper than speech) require serious navigation skills. At times, the ability to move easily between cultures can even be a matter of survival!

As you wade into the ocean of multicultural ministry as a catechetical leader, the image of an iceberg may be a useful metaphor. Like an iceberg, only a small portion of culture is manifested above the waterline. That is, the dimensions that we perceive with our senses—physical features, clothing, posture, sounds, aromas—are easy clues to culture. We associate with culture variations in music, food, hand gestures, language, spatial distance in casual settings, and other observable characteristics.

But, like an iceberg, the bulk of cultural indicators lie hidden deep below the surface. These tacit elements are not dormant, just unperceived. From visual clues alone, many cultural markers are nearly imperceptible. While the manifestation of attitudes, values, mores, and religious beliefs may be seen, they may not be accurately interpreted or understood. This hidden reality of culture, animated below the waterline and eclipsed by our own cultural biases, can trigger unintentional missteps with others.

What Is the Role of Culture in Faith Formation?

For starters, it is significant to note that Jesus, human in every way but for sin, navigated the world through the lens of a culture: the Jewish culture of the Middle East at a time of Roman occupation. The Church teaches that Jesus' experience reflected God's will and plan for all of humanity and for all faith formation:

> Since persons can only achieve their full humanity by means of culture, the Catholic Church in the United States embraces the rich cultural pluralism of all the faithful, encourages the distinctive identity of each cultural group, and urges mutual enrichment. At the same time, the Catholic Church promotes a unity of faith within the multicultural diversity of the people. (*NDC*, #11C)

In addition, catechetical leaders—and all disciples of Christ—are commanded to do more than evangelize individuals. We are called to participate in the evangelization of culture, also known as *inculturation* (a theological term). The *National Directory for Catechesis* clarifies what this means: "The Gospel is intended for every people and nation; it finds a home in every culture. . . . [Evangelization today] demands both the inculturation of the Gospel and the transformation of the culture by the Gospel. . . . It is also directed to all human cultures so that they might be open to the Gospel and live in harmony with Christian values" (*NDC*, #17A). Here we might underscore the notion that *all cultures* need to be transformed by the Gospel. The idea of a hierarchy of cultures is not supported by Catholic teaching.

Working together amid the plurality of cultures in the United States presents persistent challenges within society and inside the Church. This multicultural plurality, notwithstanding the range of lifestyle choices, the spectrum of religious beliefs even within the Catholic corral, and the growing polarization of political views and personal preferences, further complicates our ability to form a cohesive and healthy community.

What Does It Take to Walk through Closed Doors?

The Church trusts that trained catechetical leaders will transmit the tenets of faith without cultural bias. This implies the ability to echo God's word clearly, authentically, and from a core of love and respect for those being catechized: "Those who proclaim the Christian message must know and love the culture and the people to whom they bring the message for it to be able to transform the culture and the people and make them new in Christ" (*NDC*, #17A). Yet, cultural filters tend to be deeply rooted and hard to recognize, especially within ourselves.

Historically, many U.S. Catholics of other than European heritage tended to possess a dual identity, struggling to balance the cultural expression of their faith against a tide of skepticism about its religious authenticity. This dynamic persists today in many settings. A good example was Pope Benedict XVI's visit to the United States in April 2008. Some Catholic press characterized the multicultural Eucharistic celebration, which utilized sacred but nontraditional musical styles and gestures, as entertainment and as something less than true Catholic worship. While it is possible that this was merely the off-the-cuff opinion of a handful of reporters and commentators, the reality is that it voiced the silent sentiments of a host of other observers.

Too often, liturgical expressions of African, Asian, Hispanic, and indigenous cultures are deemed inappropriate for Catholic worship and are relegated to respective ethnic parishes. At times, debate about what is culturally and liturgically sound for Catholic worship can become heated and emotionally charged. As a catechetical leader, you have the opportunity to change the filter through which we approach and perceive multicultural prayer, worship, and faith formation.

Apprentice Disciples Need Catechetical Leaders to Minister Well in Culturally Diverse Settings

A 2015 USCCB study of the current state of Lay Ecclesial Ministry (LEM) was conducted by the Center for Applied Research in the Apostolate (CARA). This study found that there are more than 39,600 lay ecclesial ministers (LEMs) in the United States. The majority are engaged in religious education/formation, liturgy, music ministry, or general parish administration. Eighty percent of LEMs are women and the median age is fifty-five. The good news is that nine out of ten, or 89 percent, view their work as a vocation, not a job. "It is a call from God," they say.

The study further revealed that 88 percent of LEMs are White, 9 percent are Hispanic/Latino; less than 2 percent are Black, African American, African, Asian, or Pacific Islander; and less than 1 percent are Native American or Native Alaskan (0.2 percent). In a separate CARA study, commissioned in 2014 by the USCCB Secretariat of Cultural Diversity in the Church, it was reported that the U.S. Catholic population is 58 percent White, 34 percent Hispanic/Latino, 3 percent Black, 3 percent Asian, 1 percent Native American and Native Alaskan, and 1 percent Pacific Islander or Native Hawaiian.

Although diversity in the Church is increasing, the CARA Study of LEMs concluded that only 17 percent of LEMs believe they are prepared to work in a multicultural setting. Therefore, while demographic data indicate that more diversity in leadership could help advance the Church's mission, there is no doubt that greater intercultural competence among LEMs would be a benefit as well.

Looking beyond the numbers, more diversity and increased skill for pastoral ministry across cultural lines will help the Church in the U.S. remove some of the obstacles to evangelizing those for whom the prevailing culture represents an acquired identity. Regular encounters with people of different ethnic, religious, and ideological backgrounds can foster spiritual maturity. This may happen by simply choosing to sit in a different pew with persons you don't know or accompanying friends to events in a different parish. It may be necessary to branch out by attending cultural events in the community.

Even in settings that currently have little diversity, inculturation is applicable. As the *National Directory for Catechesis* explains, "Every culture needs to be transformed by Gospel values because the Gospel always demands a conversion of attitudes and practices wherever it is preached. Cultures must often be purified and restored in Christ" (*NDC*, #21A).

Plan *With*, Not *For*, People

So, how can we as catechetical leaders prepare ourselves to minister in multicultural settings? One way to get started is to intentionally plan and implement a multicultural parish experience, such as a prayer service, Unity Mass, or intercultural celebration. For instance, the parish feast day may offer a prime opportunity to celebrate or promote the unity of diversity within the parish. Before any planning begins, it is crucial to invite representatives from all the groups present in your location. A liturgist who is trained and experienced in multicultural pastoral settings could provide sound guidance for generating inclusive prayers, appropriate cultural rituals, and related elements. Here are some examples of dates and saints that could provide a context for multicultural events and observances.

January	August
New Year's Day	Our Lady of Czestochowa
World Day of Peace	
National Migration Week	
Birthday of Rev. Dr. Martin Luther King Jr.	
Chinese New Year (January or February)	
February	**September/October**
Valentine's Day	National Hispanic Heritage Month
Black History Month	Korean Martyrs
Mardi Gras	Indigenous Peoples' Day
Saint Paul Miki and Companions	
Saint Josephine Bakhita	
March/April	**November**
Saint Patrick	All Saints Day
Saint Joseph's Table	Día de los Muertos (All Souls)
Easter	Saint Martin de Porres
	Feast of Christ the King
	Thanksgiving
May/June	**December**
Pentecost	Feast of Our Lady of Guadalupe
Juneteenth (commemoration of the end of slavery in the U.S.)	Las Posadas
	Saint Juan Diego
	Simbang Gabi
	Christmas
	Kwanzaa
July	Other: Feast of the patron saint of the parish or annual parish gathering
Saint Junipero Serra	
Saint Kateri Tekakwitha	

As we prepare special events, we should strive for authenticity.

Evangelization loses much of its force and effectiveness if it does not take into consideration the actual people to whom it is addressed, if it does not use their language, their signs and symbols, if it does not answer the questions they ask, and if it does not have an impact on their concrete life. But on the other hand, evangelization risks losing its power and risks disappearing altogether if one empties or adulterates its content under the pretext of translating it. (*EN*, #63)

Effective multicultural initiatives always rely on thoughtful planning. When treading into multicultural waters, it is important to avoid tokenism. For instance, think beyond ethnic food and music; seek out diverse presenters and topics with broad appeal. The room environment, presentation methodology, resources chosen, and even the selection of vendors and exhibitors all communicate a commitment to reaching a diverse audience. In addition, always keep the end in mind. Is the goal prayer, liturgy, a formation experience, or something else? Remaining focused on the purpose of the event is essential.

Understanding the Catholic Experience through Diverse Cultural Expressions: An Overview

Here are a few thumbnail sketches of key ethnic groups that make up just a portion of the diverse Catholic Church today.

- **European.** Since arriving in the early sixteenth century in what is now Florida, immigrants primarily from Europe have fueled Catholicism to become the largest Christian denomination in the United States. In the nineteenth century, Catholic immigrants from Ireland, Germany, Italy, and various Eastern European countries built a complex infrastructure of parishes, schools, hospitals, universities, and orphanages to nourish and sustain the Catholic way of life. They also brought with them various ethnic devotions and practices, as well as veneration of national saints and, of course, the Blessed Virgin Mary. Catholicism in the United States became synonymous with Saint Patrick's Day, Saint Joseph's Table, May Crowning, Corpus

Christi processions, Confraternity of Christian Doctrine (CCD) classes, and the *Baltimore Catechism.*

As the prevailing culture for nearly two centuries, the European-Catholic style of worship, music, and artwork has long been assumed as the standard, the conventional yardstick, in American Catholicism. However, it is neither monolithic nor static. As discussed in chapter 2, cultural distinctions based on country of origin were evident as early immigrants (European American Catholics) were ministered to by their own ethnic clergy and religious communities. European Americans tend to have an individualistic nature, meaning that the rights and identity of the individual generally take precedence over those of the group. Over the decades, while these cultural distinctions began to fade and European Catholics blended into American culture, the European style of prayer and worship remained dominant for Catholics.

Today, European American Catholics no longer are the majority in the Catholic Church in the United States, having been surpassed by new immigrants, most notably Catholics of Hispanic and Latino heritage. The challenge of today's catechetical leader is to embrace the work of inculturation to ensure that all of God's people find their place at the table of the Lord.

- **Hispanic/Latino.** The USCCB reminds us that until recent decades, "People with roots in Latin American countries have lived in the United States from its very beginnings. However, their presence on the national scene was practically invisible" (*Hispanic/Latino Presence in the USA and the Church*, Alejandro Aguilera-Titus, MA, and Allan Figueroa Deck, SJ, PhD). In fact, according to CARA research:

- There are over 30 million Hispanic Catholics in the United States today, which represents nearly 40 percent of adult Catholics.
- Hispanics/Latinos account for 40 percent of all growth in registered parishioners in Catholic parishes in recent years.
- Latinos make up approximately 60 percent of U.S. Catholics under the age of thirty.
- Only about 10 percent of Lay Ecclesial Ministers self-identify as Hispanic/Latino.
- Fortunately, nearly 45 percent of people currently enrolled in lay-minister formation programs self-identify as Hispanic/Latino.
- Just over a quarter of U.S. parishes serve Hispanic/Latino Catholic communities (most numerous in the South and West and in urban areas of the Midwest and Northeast).

Fortunately, since the 1970s a more comprehensive pastoral approach to serving Hispanic/Latino Catholics in the U.S. has taken shape, spearheaded by *Encuentro,* a process of encountering Christ in one another. The leadership-formation initiative has enabled Hispanic Catholics to explore and articulate their place in the U.S. Church.

So what does all of this mean for you as a catechetical leader? It means, first and foremost, that you are called to a greater awareness, sensitivity, and knowledge of Hispanic culture, including the needs, hopes, dreams, and gifts of the Hispanic community. Your overriding goal is the integration of those gifts into every facet of parish life. In your ministry to Hispanics/ Latinos, you will need to integrate the following principles:

- A welcoming and hospitable spirit and a willingness to immerse yourself in the culture

- Sensitivity to unique cultural norms of various and diverse Hispanic/Latino peoples (Mexican, Cuban, Central American, Puerto Rican, and so on)
- Understanding and affirmation of common devotions and pious practices such as blessings, *posadas, novenas, quinceañeras, Día de los Muertos*, home altars, and *las mañanitas* in honor of Our Lady of Guadalupe, just to name a few
- Proactive/intentional recruitment, training, and formation of Hispanics for various leadership roles in the faith-formation program/parish
- An emphasis on an intergenerational/family-centered approach (known as *catequesis familiar*) to support the central role of the family in Hispanic culture. Families desire and need spaces where they can gather to share their stories and traditions.
- A relational approach with an emphasis on small Christian communities for adult faith formation
- The inclusion of Spanish language/bilingual options for gatherings and communications

Latino culture is festive, visual, and relational. Think fiesta! Picture family and friends sharing food, music, and laughter. It reflects a spirituality that has been characterized as home-centered, devotional, and transmitted through popular movements. Hispanics have a deep and passionate devotion to Jesus, the Blessed Mother, and the saints. Their faith is highly incarnational—meaning that they experience God in an intimate and affective manner and in the details of daily living. Likewise, Hispanics in general are not accustomed to systematic faith formation but rather faith formation related to sacramental preparation, which means that you and your program will need to be characterized by flexibility (no "one size fits all" approach).

A significant resource to assist you in catechesis in the Hispanic community is the Federation for Catechesis with Hispanics (FCH; fchcatechesis.org). FCH was formed in 2013 (growing out of the Forum for Catechesis with Hispanics) and was approved by the National Conference for Catechetical Leadership (NCCL) Board to become the first federation in NCCL. It is a focus-specific group of NCCL members, national in scope, existing to enhance and strengthen the Conference mission and to better serve the needs of Hispanic Catholics.

Finally, when it comes to serving as a leader in the Hispanic/Latino community, the following ten leadership principles proposed by Juana Bordas—blogger, leader, writer, teacher, and president of Mestiza Leadership International—are very helpful:

1. [**Buen carácter**]—a leader must be a person of character, humility, and integrity so that he or she may be worthy of people's trust and loyalty.

2. **Conciencia**—a leader must have depth and core values and be motivated by a sincere desire to serve others.

3. [**Llamado**]—a leader must have a sense of personal and collective purpose and destiny, or "calling."

4. **La cultura**—a leader must have an understanding of the shared values, wisdom, and common history, heritage, and traditions of the people he or she serves.

5. **De colores**—a leader must be committed to bringing together diverse communities in order to build a shared identity; inclusiveness is not optional.

6. **Juntos**—a leader must have a solidarity with the people he or she serves, a "we are together" approach that is manifested through stewardship.

7. **¡Adelante!**—a leader must have a global vision with an immigrant spirit that manifests itself through social justice and a desire to bring unity without assimilation.

8. **Sí, se puede**—a leader must be a coalition builder, an advocate with the heart and soul of an activist and an attitude characterized by hopeful optimism.

9. **Gozar la vida**—a leader must be one who is congenial and celebrates life, mirroring the celebratory and festive nature of Hispanic people.

10. **Fe y esperanza**—a leader must be one who embodies and inspires faith and hope, recognizing that it is spirituality that sustains and upholds all activities and activism. There is no separation between faith and daily living.

- **Asian and Pacific Islander (API).** Today, APIs are the fastest-growing group in the United States; however, it is important to note that the term "Asian/Pacific Islander" includes a huge diversity of ethnicities and countries of origin—Chinese, Korean, Filipino, Japanese, Indian, Vietnamese, Pakistani, Hawaiian, and many more. Nearly three out of five APIs were born abroad. In most API countries, Catholics are a minority faith, the exception being Filipinos, who constitute the largest group of APIs in the U.S. The second-largest groups are Vietnamese and Chinese. In a report prepared for the USCCB Secretariat for Cultural Diversity in the Church in 2015, one respondent in the study likened the reality of API to a patchwork quilt:

> The quilt is made up of different patches of fabric and those different patches of fabric are all the different people within that Vietnamese, Korean, Filipino, Cambodian, Samoan, Chinese type of community, whatever API community you want to put on that label. So within the API community,

although you might see a lot of similarities, each one is a
different piece of fabric making up an intricate quilt. What
we've seen all together and formed some consistency in that
unity are the threads, and those threads are those shared
sacramental and practices. . . . Those are the threads that
[combine] all those members of those communities together
and [hold] them together. (Tricia C. Bruce, PhD, Jerry Z.
Park, PhD, and Stephen M. Cherry, PhD, *Asian and Pacific
Island Catholics in the United States*, 11)

API cultures and spirituality tend to be collectivist and have a
high regard for group harmony over the needs and wishes of
individuals, which is often in stark contrast to the individualist
emphasis of prevailing American culture. A respondent to the
study described this collectivist nature in the following manner:
"They are much more concerned with making sure everybody's
getting along and things are going smoothly and things like that.
When there is conflict, they will be quiet most often to keep
peace and so that people can work together" (12).

According to the study, while 83 percent of respondents speak
a language other than English at home, most are bilingual. This
results in pastoral practice that is often bilingual. For example,
confessions may be heard in English, but the penitent may pray
the Act of Contrition in his or her native tongue. This diversity
and flexibility are crucial to communicating to people that their
culture is sacred. It is likewise imperative for you as a catechetical
leader to learn how various API communities understand the
concepts of leadership and conflict in order to avoid
miscommunications.

Like other ethnic groups, various API Catholics hold a wide
variety of ethnic celebrations honoring apparitions of Mary, as
well as regional and national saints and ancestors. In addition,

various devotional practices and popular piety are of great importance to API Catholics. Their worldview can often be characterized as more spiritual/supernatural than that of their counterparts in Western cultures. APIs also tend to embody a very steadfast loyalty to the Church and its official teachings and traditionally exhibit higher rates of Mass attendance and involvement in ministries than other ethnic groups. Finally, prayer groups also play a significant role in the lives of APIs, as do music and food!

As a catechetical leader, it is important to know that Catholics of Asian and Pacific Island origins desire to faithfully transmit not only the Catholic faith to succeeding generations but also ethnic traditions that are tied to their expression of Catholicism.

- **African.** The presence of Black Catholics in the U.S. dates from the earliest settlements in St. Augustine (1565), Maryland (1634), and elsewhere. Currently, there are 3 million Catholics of African descent in the U.S. About 76 percent of them belong to shared (multicultural) parishes. Only 24 percent worship in historically, predominantly African American parishes. According to Catholic scholar Fr. Bryan N. Massingale, for too long, efforts to bring Black cultural expression into the U.S. Church have been met with suspicion, anxiety, and even fear and hostility—reactions that are not present when European cultural expressions merge with Catholicism. As Msgr. Ray East explains it, to be a Black Catholic in the United States is to be "a minority within a minority" (Msgr. Ray East, interview on African American Catholic spirituality in *U.S. Catholic*, March 2014).

  The term *Black Catholics* includes those of Caribbean descent and those native to Africa. Yet the majority of Black Catholics are of African descent, with roots in the U.S. dating back to the African diaspora that was fueled primarily by the slave trade. Rooted in this history, Black Catholic spirituality is grounded in the gift of freedom in Jesus Christ and characterized by gratitude for this great gift. In his article "Ministry in the Black Catholic Community," Reverend Scott A. Bailey emphasizes the need for a deeper understanding of Black history and culture among those in leadership roles in the Black Catholic community. Scripture—stories that have nourished and maintained faith and hope during times of oppression and pain—is at the heart of Black spirituality. The stories of Israel's experience of bondage and liberation resonate deeply with the experience of Black Catholics in the United States. This reverence for the word of God in Scripture coincides with a style of preaching that is uniquely and powerfully scriptural and easily applied to daily living.

As a result of this emphasis on gratitude for the gift of freedom in Jesus Christ, Black Catholic spirituality is characterized by great hope and joy! This is often expressed and articulated in song, dance, colorful clothing, and dynamic preaching. According to Msgr. East, Black Catholics insist on a religion they can "feel" (Msgr. Ray East, interview on African American Catholic spirituality). He goes on to describe Black Catholic spirituality as being welcoming, unitive, holistic, contemplative, and spirit-built, with a passion for justice.

In *What We Have Seen and Heard: A Pastoral Letter on Evangelization from the Black Bishops of the United States*, the bishops write,

> There is a richness in our Black experience that we must share with the entire People of God. These are gifts that are part of an African past. For we have heard with Black ears and we have seen with Black eyes and we have understood with an frican heart. We thank God for the gifts of our Catholic ith and we give thanks for the gifts of our Blackness. In all

humility we turn to the whole Church that it might share our gifts so that "our joy may be complete."

As a catechetical leader, the goal of your service to Black Catholics should be to ensure that their experience will be "truly Black and authentically Catholic" and that the gifts of the Black Catholic community may enrich the Church as a whole. The following are some of the principles for you to apply as a catechetical leader in service to the Black Catholic community:

1. Ministry that is fueled by an evangelizing spirit and a spirit of joy that must be shared

2. An emphasis on the word of God/Scripture and the great liberating story of salvation history

3. A focus on liberating people from various forms of oppression and racism and working for justice and reconciliation

4. Emphasis on the centrality of prayer and contemplation

5. A comfort with expressions of faith that are holistic, combining the head (firmly intellectual) and the heart (deeply affective)

6. An emphasis on family (extended family) and community

7. A spirit of ecumenism and an understanding/appreciation of the concept of "The Black Church," which crosses denominational boundaries

8. Intentional and proactive efforts to call forth, train, and form leaders in the Black Catholic community

9. A wide variety of opportunities for Black youth, who are especially vulnerable in today's society

10. A familiarity with the Rite of Christian Initiation for Adults (RCIA) as a vehicle for evangelization

11. Uplifting worship opportunities that are truly a time for praise and thanksgiving and are authentic expressions of spiritual vitality

12. The inclusion (in stories and images) of saints (small *s* and large *S*) of color, such as Augustus Tolton, Martin de Porres, Josephine Bakhita, Mother Mary Lange, Pierre Toussaint, Charles Lwanga, Perpetua and Felicity, Sr. Thea Bowman, and others

(Adapted from *What We Have Seen and Heard: A Pastoral Letter on Evangelization from the Black Bishops of the United States*, [St. Anthony Messenger Press, 1984])

- **Indigenous Peoples.** This cultural family includes American Indians, Native Alaskans, and Mayans. Native Americans suffered greatly at the hands of European powers, often in the name of the Church. Many of these same powers also punished numerous priests, sisters, and laypeople who spoke out against the crimes committed against indigenous peoples. This history has not made it easy for Native Americans to feel totally at home in the Catholic Church. In 1992, to commemorate the 500th anniversary of Columbus's coming to this part of the world, the United States Conference of Catholic Bishops' Ad Hoc Committee on Native American Catholics issued a letter acknowledging the need for hope in the face of a painful past: "1992: A Time for Remembering, Reconciling, and Recommitting Ourselves as a People."

In 2002, the same committee issued a report entitled "Native American Catholics at the Millennium." This report indicated that approximately 20–25 percent of Native Americans are Catholic and that approximately one-half of all Native Americans in the U.S. "live in dioceses that have no office or program specifically designed to meet their needs." In addition, critical issues in many Native American communities include mass incarceration, poverty, joblessness, ongoing loss of land and identity (including native languages), exploitation of natural resources, domestic violence, lack of education, overcrowding, and inadequate health care.

In catechetical ministry to Native American Catholics, the major issues include inculturation, worship, and sacraments. Today, Native American Catholics celebrate their faith with a blend of traditional Catholicism and Native American customs and symbols. This may include colorful tribal attire, drumming, dancing, smudging (blessing or purifying with cedar, sage, etc.), eagle feathers used in blessings, vision quests, sweat lodges, pipe-smoking, four-directional prayer (turning to the north, south, east, and west), and sacred vestments and vessels with Native designs. Native American Catholics practice a spirituality that is closely tied to nature and is steeped in rituals and ceremonies. For Native American Catholics, it is crucial for them to recognize their own culture incorporated into Catholic ritual.

In 2010, Saint Kateri Tekakwitha was canonized as the first Native American saint. The Tekakwitha Conference is the "Voice, Presence and Identity of Indigenous Catholics of North America under the protection and inspiration of Saint Kateri Tekakwitha." The conference publishes and provides Native American Catholic catechetical resources and has been hosting an annual conference since 1939. Their newsletter, *Cross and Feathers*, is available on their Web site (tekconf.org).

- **New Immigrants.** This group comprises first-generation immigrants from all continents, unlike earlier immigrants who came primarily from Europe. The Church is concerned with and uniquely challenged by the pastoral needs of migrants, refugees, travelers, and those seeking asylum. Commonly, people emigrate in reaction to grave threats of war, violence, ethnic targeting, and severe poverty. Many new immigrants to the U.S. are Catholic. They are the source of many religious vocations servicing the Church in the United States today.

Admittedly, immigration is a volatile topic of conversation. However, the Church honors the dignity of every person. As the U.S. Catholic bishops stated in *Welcoming the Stranger Among Us: Unity in Diversity* (November 2000), "We call upon all people of good will, but Catholics especially, to welcome the newcomers in their neighborhoods and schools, in their places of work and worship, with heartfelt hospitality, openness, and eagerness both to help and to learn from our brothers and sisters, of whatever race, religion, ethnicity, or background."

Use the Front-Door Key

The concepts of "Individualist" and "Collectivist" cultures is a revealing means of understanding what transpires in intercultural settings such as the parish, workplace, and learning environments. These concepts can become a useful "key" to unlock our differences and help us interpret the dynamics of relationships within different cultures. Naturally, this spectrum of perspectives may vary in individuals and groups.

More than two-thirds of the world's cultures are Collectivist, operating mostly in Africa, Asia, and Latin America. In a Collectivist culture, the group has priority over the individual. Individualist cultures, which make up less than one-third of the global population, are endemic to the prevailing culture of the United States, Europe, and Canada. The Individualist culture values the person over the group. As a catechetical leader, you will find that some ethnic groups are naturally intergenerational (the entire family—including little children as well as grandparents, aunts, and uncles—will show up for a faith-formation experience). This fact may require intentional efforts on your part to frame a formation experience as intergenerational.

This fundamental distinction is one example of the hidden realities identified in the iceberg metaphor we examined earlier. Opposing perspectives and motivations may surface in intercultural communications, decision making, event planning, and learning situations. For instance, it is common for people in some ethnic groups to respond yes, when they really mean, "I don't want to offend you, but . . . no." This might explain why some people will say yes to your invitation to participate in a catechetical event but then simply not show up. Being aware of these cultural assumptions will help you unlock your creativity as you minister to them.

Or, Use the Hidden Spare Key

We human beings, created in the image and likeness of our Triune God, are "wired" for relationships with other people. Humans naturally want others to view them favorably. We all want to put forward a good "face." This truth is another key to understanding different cultures.

Dr. Stella Ting-Toomey, a researcher in intercultural communications and conflict management, developed *The Matrix of Face: An Updated Face-Negotiation Theory*. She observes, "Face is the public image of a group . . . how a group wants other individuals and groups to see it" (*Building Intercultural Competence for Ministers*, 2012). Ting-Toomey identifies three basic values that are important to all cultural/ethnic groups as they interact with other groups:

- Autonomy—My group is self-sufficient.
- Morality—My group is likeable, reliable, approachable.
- Competent—My group has resources and achievements.

In intercultural communication, groups have different approaches to saving (protecting) face or giving (projecting) face in ways that will show they are autonomous, moral, and competent. For example, in some cultures, compromising may be a face-giving maneuver, and using self-deprecating language may be a face-saving strategy. You can use these underlying values as a "spare key" to open doors of effective ministry among ethnic groups.

Inculturation and Mercy

In many ways, inculturation only becomes an issue when we encounter people whom we view as different from ourselves. When such encounters occur, inculturation invites us to ask ourselves, "How is God already present among this group of people?" as well as, "How can I best proclaim God's presence to this group of people?" When we encounter people we view as different than ourselves, often we find that there are not only racial differences but also socioeconomic differences. This is especially true when we encounter those who are in extreme poverty, those who are homeless, and those who lack the necessities of life such as food, clothing, and shelter—those Jesus referred to as the "least" of our brothers and sisters (Mt 25:40). It was with this in mind that the late Cardinal Francis George, OMI, famously told a group of wealthy benefactors, "The poor need you to draw them out of their poverty, and you need the poor to keep you out of hell." By that, he meant that we need the poor to remind us of God's presence in those whom society seems to have forgotten. In other words, those who are marginalized by society play a crucial role in the reality that is catechesis, for it is through learning and practicing works of mercy for those in need that we encounter Jesus Christ in a most powerful way.

The corporal and spiritual works of mercy are not just lists to be memorized but actions that Catholics are taught to incorporate into daily living. It is for this reason that catechetical programs must integrate opportunities for children, teens, and adults to engage in works of mercy to serve those in need. If catechesis is truly an apprenticeship into a way of life, as the *General Directory for Catechesis* describes it, then this way of life must be characterized by ongoing engagement in works of mercy. If this apprenticeship is to be truly effective, we must not wait until children reach the age of confirmation and then require them to perform a minimum number of service hours or a service project. Mercy is not a project to be completed or a task to be crossed off of a list—it is a way of encountering Jesus in our neighbors. For that reason, I would go as far as to recommend that such opportunities be referred to as "mercy experiences" rather than service projects.

The truth is, many other institutions, including public schools, require completion of a service component as a civics lesson/experience. While I'm not suggesting that the service we do in the name of the Church is better, the fact is, we do service for a different reason. People do service for a number of reasons: to pay it forward, to feel good about themselves, out of a sense of compassion for others, because of a personal tie to a cause, and so on. These are all good. Followers of Jesus, however, serve others to make the kingdom of God visible to those on the brink of despair. We do service to bring hope to others. We do service to bring glory to God. We do service to encounter Jesus. We do not perform good works to please or assuage God. We do not do good works to earn grace or salvation. We do good works because God is love and we yearn to live in God. By sharing love with others, we encounter the living God. One important way to distinguish works of mercy from service hours is by making sure that prayer and reflection are a part of the experience, before, during, and after.

Mercy experiences can take many forms, ranging from volunteering at a soup kitchen, a homeless shelter, or a food pantry (for more mature learners) to making care packages for people who are homeless, creating get-well cards for the sick and homebound, and preparing sandwiches for those who can't afford a meal. Such activities are also conducive to parent and family involvement. With regards to the overall catechetical program, it is important to remember that mercy experiences are not an interruption in your faith-formation schedule but are part and parcel of apprenticing others into a life of discipleship.

Inculturation and Justice

As soon as we venture into the realm of extending charity and sharing mercy with those in need, we come to recognize that there are often societal factors to blame for their misfortune. It is for this reason that the Church refers to charity and justice as the "two feet" of social action. It is not enough that we perform works of mercy to alleviate the suffering of others: we are also called to transform those societal realities that deprive people of enjoying the abundance of God's creation.

For centuries, the Catholic Church has been developing a body of work (papal encyclicals, apostolic exhortations, and various Church documents) that has formed what is now known as "Catholic social teaching." When St. Ignatius of Loyola founded the Jesuits back in the sixteenth century, he believed firmly that faith must be put into action and called his followers to be "people for others." Nearly four hundred years later, one of his successors, Fr. Pedro Arrupe, SJ (Jesuit Superior General, 1965–1983) said, "We cannot separate action for justice from the proclamation of the Word of God." Think this idea is radical? Jesus taught this principle over two thousand years ago! In his Parable of the Last Judgment, Jesus made it abundantly clear that faith in him will be judged by how well that faith was put into action:

> Then the righteous will answer him, "Lord, when did we see thee hungry and feed thee, or thirsty and give thee drink? And when did we see thee a stranger and welcome thee, or naked and clothe thee? And when did we see thee sick or in prison and visit thee?" And the King will answer them, "Truly, I say to you, as you did it

to one of the least of these my brethren, you did it to me." (Mat. 25:37–40, RSV)

In other words, faith formation strives to create people for others. To guide us in this endeavor, the bishops of the United States wrote *Sharing Catholic Social Teaching: Challenges and Directions*, which outlines seven principles of social justice in Catholic teaching. By following these principles, we will discover how to live as people for others.

- Dignity of the Human Person—We are called to ask whether our actions as a society respect or threaten the life and dignity of the human person.

- Call to Family, Community, and Participation—We are called to support the family—the principle social institution—so that people can participate in society, build a community spirit, and promote the well-being of all.

- Rights and Responsibilities—We are called to protect the rights that all people have to those things required for a decent human life, such as food, clothing, and shelter.

- Option for the Poor and Vulnerable—We are called to pay special attention to the needs of those who are poor.

- Dignity of Work and the Rights of Workers—We are called to protect the basic rights of all workers: the right to engage in productive work, fair wages, and private property and the right to organize, join unions, and pursue economic opportunity.

- Solidarity—We are called to recognize that, because God is our Father, we are all brothers and sisters, with the responsibility to care for one another.

- Care for God's Creation—We are called to care for all that God has made.

In the Parable of the Last Judgment, Jesus makes clear our responsibility to tend to the needs of others. The Church teaches this responsibility in these seven principles of Catholic social teaching, reminding us that, if we want to live as followers of Jesus, we need to live as people for others. Ultimately, inculturation calls us to roll up our sleeves and get to work, extending God's mercy to those in need and working to transform society so that all people may enjoy the abundance of God's creation. Mercy and justice are not "electives" in the school of discipleship; they are course "requirements."

Summary: And the Word Became Flesh

The Word became flesh
and made his dwelling among us,
and we saw his glory,
the glory as of the Father's only Son,
full of grace and truth. (John 1:14, NABRE)

According to the *NDC,* "Jesus Christ is the human face of God and the divine face of humanity. The incarnation of the only Son of God is the original inculturation of God's word" (#21A). Jesus, our perfect model of evangelization for the world, is always with us as a guide as we remain disciples-in-training. Somewhere in the commitment to continue growing spiritually, the apprentice is transformed. Then the head, heart, and hands open to receive diversity as a gift rather than a burden.

For Reflection and Discussion

Discuss the following set of questions with a trusted friend or colleague:

- What is your primary culture? Perhaps you identify with multiple cultures, e.g., gender, birth generation, region or country of birth, professional association, even hobbies or entertainment preferences. Name them.

- What is your cultural or ethnic heritage? What role, if any, does this play in your view of yourself?
- How do you feel when others call out their cultural heritage? Have you ever made a cultural faux pas? How do you feel about that conversation?

Growing as a Catechetical Leader

Understanding inculturation, acting on it, and cultivating intercultural competence may feel like just one more thing to do! However, this is not another box to check. It is woven throughout all Seven Tasks of Catechesis (*NDC*, #21A). Culturally speaking, we are like fish in water. We do not realize we are seeing situations through our own cultural lens until we hit an obstacle, such as a major miscommunication or unin-

tended hurt feelings. One of the great features of being human is the ability to change our thinking and behavior in line with the will of God. Regardless of our past circumstances and present conditions, God wants to transform our hearts and increase our capacity to love our Creator (whom we don't see) and the sisters and brothers we see before us who are made in God's image and likeness. What life experiences have prepared you for catechetical leadership in a multicultural setting? Conversely, what situations in your life have hindered your ability to acquire the knowledge, skills, and attitudes needed to catechize others in a multicultural setting?

Go to www.loyolapress.com/ECL to access the worksheet.

Suggested Action

Quickly answer True or False to the following statements. Don't over-think the statements. Then, focus on one or two statements that challenge you, and elaborate on your answers.

	True	False
1. I understand *catholic* to mean "universal" and to include all ethnic groups without distinction.		
2. I believe we are all God's children and should be treated the same.		
3. I see people, not their color.		
4. Our parish welcomes all people regardless of their birth country or immigration status.		
5. The leadership in our parish reflects the diversity in our diocese.		
6. I belong to a shared parish.		
7. When I talk about race, I feel fear, ignorance, and/or guilt.		
8. I never discuss race.		
9. I believe that discussing racial and ethnic differences causes or exacerbates division.		
10. A visitor from another planet could see that our parish values cultural diversity.		

For Further Consideration

Asian and Pacific Island Catholics in the United States. Tricia C. Bruce, PhD, Jerry Z. Park, PhD, and Stephen M. Cherry, PhD (Washington, DC: United States Conference of Catholic Bishops, October 2015).

Best Practices for Shared Parishes: So That They May All Be One (Washington, DC: United States Conference of Catholic Bishops, 2013).

Building Intercultural Competence for Ministers (Washington, DC: United States Conference of Catholic Bishops, 2012).

Hispanic/Latino Presence in the USA and the Church. Alejandro Aguilera-Titus, MA, and Allan Figueroa Deck, SJ, PhD (Washington, DC: United States Council of Catholic Bishops, 1992, 2002).

Native American Catholics at the Millennium (Washington, DC: United States Conference of Catholic Bishops, 2002).

"What We Have Seen and Heard: A Pastoral Letter on Evangelization from the Black Bishops of the United States" (Washington, DC: United States Conference of Catholic Bishops, 1984).

http://www.usccb.org/issues-and-action/cultural-diversity/.

4

It All Begins at Home: Catechesis, the Family, and the Domestic Church

Back in the Day, Long Ago . . .

Once upon a time, families gathered at the kitchen table for a common meal. They "said grace" together, talked about the happenings of the day at work, school, home, and extracurricular activities. Meatless Fridays were customary for Catholics. Family members might observe one another praying, whether it was with children at bedtime, while Mother was occupied with household tasks, or during a contemplative moment for Dad.

Back in the day, faith-building tools for the family were simple: Catholic prayers, the prescribed menu of questions and answers found in the *Baltimore Catechism*, the Rosary. Memorizing doctrinal formulas, such as the Apostles' Creed, the Ten Commandments, the Three Theological Virtues, and the Seven Deadly Sins, began at an early age. Despite likely theological gaps, a fundamental love for God was encouraged within the family and reinforced through schools and the wider community.

The *Catechism of the Catholic Church* teaches that "the Christian home is the place where children receive the first proclamation of the faith. For this reason the family home is rightly called 'the domestic church,' a community of grace and prayer, a school of human virtues and of Christian charity" (*CCC*, #1666). In a former era, tough questions about faith were "answered" with the mantra "It is a mystery." Faith was imprinted more firmly through behavior than by religious instruction. Essentially, faith was transmitted and gradually adopted through devotional practices and rituals within the family, both at home and in public.

Many families developed their own traditions around liturgical seasons and parish activities. For example, a family might place a homemade Advent wreath in a prominent spot in their home. Older Catholics remember that in May (the month of Mary) and October (the month of the Holy Rosary), their parents or grandparents called them in from play in order to recite the Rosary on their knees as a family. Of course, children knew to keep any objections hidden or they soon learned their lesson!

There were Saturday afternoon trips to the confessional, and the process of laying out one's "Sunday best" and beginning preparations for Sunday dinner. Then the scurrying to get everyone up and dressed on time for Sunday Mass. It all signaled the importance of observing the Sabbath.

Children's assignments from religion class or CCD might become a family affair, as instructions likely invited parental participation. In her book *The Great Emergence: How Christianity Is Changing and Why* (Baker Books, 2008, 2012), the late, great Phyllis Tickle described how, in a bygone era, the family would gather at Grandma's house on Sunday afternoon, and "it was Grandma, in general, who asked . . . exactly what Johnny had learned in Sunday School" (86–87). Youth whose older relatives served as lectors, choir members, ushers, sodalists, and knights were recruited to be altar servers and helpers in the church. To hold the paten, ring the bells, sing in the choir, place flowers on the altar—responsibilities like these drew young people into the action of believers and frequently nurtured interest in the things of God.

In those days the home environment played a strong supporting role as an agent of faith transmission. Elements of church that were transported to the home served as messengers of faith: a crucifix on a bedroom wall, holy statues in the living room, and sacred art on the dining room wall were visible fixtures in many Catholic homes. One's visiting friends could find prayer cards on an end table, a rosary hanging from a headboard or tucked under a pillow. In the kitchen, one might spot a parish bulletin tacked to the refrigerator or an image of the Blessed Mother on the ledge of a kitchen window between the small plants.

We Cannot Turn Back Time; However . . .

Within some families, this messaging may have felt like overkill for some members, while it anchored and bolstered the faith of others. We cannot turn back time, nor would most of us want to go back for various reasons. However, contemporary American lifestyles are vastly different, changed by a variety of factors over the past century. Phyllis Tickle explains that with the growing popularity of the automobile in the early twentieth century, Grandma got left behind in favor of "spins out into the countryside" (and later, the mall and sports activities), thus transforming the Sabbath into merely Sunday. This "marginalization of Grandma," according to Tickle, is just one factor that has led to the gradual erosion of the family's role in forming children in faith. As a result of this trend, the movement of faith through subsequent generations within the family has been stymied. Today, the generations differ in their understanding of God and spirituality, as John Roberto observes in *Reimagining Faith Formation for the 21st Century*.

Recently, a friend shared a concern that his son's home offers no evidence of the faith that was lovingly and intentionally given in his youth. There is no Bible, no crucifix, nor any religious article to be found. This is not to conclude that Bible or prayer apps are not downloaded to the family's mobile devices. Even so, digital tools are primarily for personal use, not readily observable by others—notably, the children.

And yet, despite all these changes, the home is still the most fruitful environment for growing the seed of faith that God plants in the hearts of his children. Family life waters, nourishes, and tests this garden of faith. As the *Catechism of the Catholic Church* explains: "The Christian family is the first place of education in prayer. Based on the sacrament of marriage, the family is the 'domestic church' where God's children learn to pray 'as the Church' and to persevere in prayer. For young children in particular, daily family prayer is the first witness of the Church's living memory as awakened patiently by the Holy Spirit" (*CCC*, #2685). Ideally, catechesis begins at home. Although it may not look exactly as it did a century ago, faith in the home is still possible and, dare I say, a nonnegotiable.

"Nothing replaces family catechesis" (*GDC,* #178). In the past, with the family and communities playing such a supportive role in faith formation, it was sufficient for families to drop their kids off at Catholic school or CCD to learn the formal aspects and doctrines of the faith. Over time, parents came to believe that Catholic schools and religious-education programs were better equipped to transmit the faith than they themselves were. As a result, far too many parents today rely totally on institutions such as Catholic schools and religious-education programs to form their children into faithful disciples. In the present economic and social environment, this weight is too great for Catholic schools and parish programs to carry (Thomas Groome, *Will There Be Faith?*).

The "Typical" American Family?

To shed further light on the contemporary challenge of family catechesis, there is no typical American family. Following are ten common ways that families are configured today:

1. Married couple with children
2. Married couple without children
3. Blended family with married couple and children from previous union(s)
4. Single parent with children
5. Unmarried couple with children
6. Unmarried couple without children
7. Same-sex couple with children
8. Same-sex couple without children
9. Grandparents and parents living together with children
10. Grandparents as primary caregivers of children
11. Parents with adult children living at home

While many of these arrangements existed in the past, some used to be considered irregular, even inconceivable and taboo. This is no longer the case. This came to light for me personally while preparing teens for confirmation. As the years progressed, fewer students lived with their biological parents. And some who did were supported in their faith development solely by a grandparent. With one group of candidates, the sponsors were more reliable than the parents. We also found that several youth invited particular adult parishioners to sponsor them for the sacrament instead of a family member. Is this consistent with your observations?

It is within *this* family context, not the family context of the 1950s, that we are called to proclaim the Good News of Jesus Christ. While families have changed, they remain the soil in which the seed of faith is planted and nurtured.

Empowering Families to Be the Domestic Church

Thus, as a catechetical leader, you are called to form not just children but entire families. Moving forward, your task is to equip and empower families to once again embrace their role as the domestic church: a place where faith takes root and is nurtured. What approaches does the twenty-first-century catechetical leader need to take to make this a reality? Let's look at a variety of strategies.

- **Flexibility.** Because families are so busy and are pulled in so many different directions, it is more important than ever to provide options and flexibility when it comes to scheduling faith-formation sessions and opportunities. While it is not humanly possible to cater to every family's individual needs and circumstances, it is important to offer options that show consideration for people's busy schedules. This is especially important when it comes to sacramental preparation. Families today no longer march in lockstep—having their children baptized as infants, bringing them to first communion in second grade and confirmation in eighth grade. Children "out of sequence" is the new normal. You need to develop and sustain a catechumenal approach to the sacraments—one that involves the whole family. This should go without saying, but it is imperative that you not shame parents for bringing their children "out of sequence." Rather, express understanding and welcome them, then enlist their full commitment in moving forward as a family to grow in faith.
- **Evangelization.** Today, it is safe to assume that a large number of parents are themselves in need of evangelization and catechesis.

Many parents nowadays do not feel confident about their capacity to guide their children's spiritual development. They may not have had as much practice as their parents had. Perhaps they didn't attend Mass regularly for many years or did not receive much explanation about the faith. More parents today are themselves children of divorce and blended families, for which weekly religious instruction was not a part of the family routine. Do all you can to welcome, invite, and engage parents in ways that were not needed a generation or two ago. Offer them every opportunity to grow in their own faith and to be evangelized through encounters with Christ.

- **"New" Methods.** Many parishes are turning to faith-formation programs that can be described as "family catechesis." This is an approach that combines monthly intergenerational gatherings (including time together as a family and an opportunity for adult faith formation while children attend a session with their catechist) with at-home sessions for children and their parents to work on together. In many ways, this approach is not new at all, since it simply calls upon parents to embrace their responsibility to teach their children in the faith. What is different is the time spent forming the adults and equipping/assisting them as they teach their own children.

- **Technology and Social Media.** To foster better communication with families, it is imperative for you to use the latest technology and social-media formats, not only to share information about logistics, dates, and times but also as vehicles for faith formation per se. For example, you can utilize video meetings, using Skype or FaceTime on your computer or smartphone, to deliver brief inspirational/catechetical messages to parents. This will help them learn more about their own faith as they lead their children to a deeper faith. Likewise, because families are so busy and are pulled in many different directions, it's important for you to be able to provide catechetical experiences digitally for those who cannot attend classes.

- **Listening.** Part of your job as a catechetical leader is to actively and compassionately listen. As individuals, couples, or families share their stories (many of which will be very complex), you will get to know them so you can better serve them. Your role is not simply to administer a program but also to minister *to people*. While you are not a counselor or therapist, you are a pastoral minister who must seek to heal wounds and bring people closer to Christ. Often, that process begins simply by providing a listening ear. Therefore, it is imperative that you learn and practice pastoral presence, which is the ability to communicate authentic concern and care by focusing your undivided attention on the person(s) you are ministering to. Such active listening is referred to as "attending," which involves positioning yourself physically so as to communicate full attention. In his book *The Skilled Helper* (Cengage Learning, 2013, 77—78), Gerard Egan offers the SOLER model.

  - **S** = SQUARELY face the person.
  - **O** = OPEN your posture by uncrossing your arms and legs.
  - **L** = LEAN toward the person occasionally.
  - **E** = Make EYE contact.
  - **R** = RELAX your body and mind.

Remember to listen not only with your ears but with your eyes and your heart as well. In other words, observe people's body language, facial expression, and tone of voice to pick up on cues that might reveal a story behind the story. Reflect back to others what you hear them saying in order to be sure you're all on the same page. The key is to always be inviting those to whom you are ministering to recognize what God might be calling them to, as you help them to assess their situation, understand it, and act upon it.

- **Equipping.** Like my friend's son, who had no religious symbols in his home, many of the parents and families you minister to have no understanding of Catholic domestic traditions, such as displaying a crucifix, a Bible, or an image of Jesus or Mary in the home. You will need to teach families about such traditions and provide them with information about where they can acquire religious symbols for their home. Likewise, equip families with practical suggestions for integrating faith into daily living. For example, in his book *Raising Faith-Filled Kids,* Tom McGrath offers forty ways to foster prayer in the home. Some of his suggestions include "Say an Our Father whenever you start a long car trip," or "Keep a prayer jar for special prayer intentions or requests," or "Find out when a family member's important meeting or test is and remember to pray at that time," just to name a few.

- **Coaching.** Parents today need assistance just learning the ins and outs of parenting. It is less common today for extended families to live together under one roof or in the same building, as a built-in support system for new parents. Many parents are completely on their own with little or no knowledge of how to go about the task of parenting. More and more catechetical leaders are coming to see themselves as "coaches" for parents—providing them with the help they need to flourish as parents who can raise their children in mind, body, and spirit.

- **Facilitating Faith-Sharing.** A crucial part of faith formation is the sharing of one's faith. It is especially critical that children hear their parents talk about their faith. In all of your catechetical programming, be sure to make it a priority to always invite parents and children to engage with one another in sharing their faith and praying together. By facilitating family faith conversations, you can help families to develop a "religiosity" that perhaps has been missing from their lives.

- **Encouraging Rituals.** Today's society is obsessed with empirical data, while our Catholic faith is an invitation to encounter mystery. That requires a different form of expression, namely, ritual. One of the most powerful ways that families can develop their own religiosity is to establish and practice family rituals, such as saying grace before meals, blessing children at bedtime and as they leave for school, reading the Bible, lighting an Advent wreath during Advent, and so on.

- **Instigating.** In his book *A Church on the Move: 52 Ways to Get Mission and Mercy in Motion*, Joe Paprocki emphasizes the need not only to indoctrinate but also to instigate when it comes to our faith. In other words, we need to mobilize people into "armies" whose task is to provide corporal and spiritual works of mercy. Families should be encouraged to participate together in mercy experiences (i.e., service opportunities) so that they come to see selfless love as the heart of discipleship.

- **Celebrating Families.** Perhaps one of the most powerful things you can do as a catechetical leader is to celebrate the many ways that families are growing in faith together. Take every opportunity to highlight families in your newsletter, on your bulletin board, and on your Web site and social-media sites. Post pictures of families in action, and invite them to witness to their faith by providing a few sentences about how a particular experience helped them to grow in faith.

A Family Faith Legacy Is Built for Efficiency . . . and Traction

Families are good at transmitting values and beliefs—political, ethical, cultural, and religious. Statistically, parents who are religiously active produce more faith-practicing disciples. Similarly, religiously unaffiliated parents generate families in which religion plays little or no role. Numerous studies show that Catholics (along with mainline Protestants) have experienced dramatic declines in religiosity and faith transmission in recent decades.

It is no secret that Americans value personal freedom and privacy. Consequently, secular thinking attempts to sustain boundaries between the family and community, as though the family were a discrete, self-contained organism. The Church, however, takes an alternative position.

> The Christian family is a communion of persons, a sign and image of the communion of the Father and the Son in the Holy Spirit. In the procreation and education of children it reflects the Father's work of creation. It is called to partake of the prayer and sacrifice of Christ. Daily prayer and the reading of the Word of God strengthen it in charity. The Christian family has an evangelizing and missionary task. (*CCC*, #2205)

God desires that families manifest the mystery of the Holy Trinity to the world in ways that individuals alone cannot. Through daily communications and the give-and-take within the family unit, this small community of persons faces countless opportunities to practice charity, patience, forgiveness, generosity, humility, perseverance, honesty, and all manner of virtue. Experiences at home are more memorable; the lessons are more lasting than the most brilliant lecture or eye-opening research project.

In addition to providing an academic education and teaching good hygiene, etiquette, and various practices that are specific to individual families, parents are responsible for their children's moral development. Pope Francis emphasizes this: "Parents are also responsible for shaping the will of their children, fostering good habits and a natural inclination to goodness. This entails presenting certain ways of thinking and acting as desirable and worthwhile, as a part of a gradual process of growth" (*Amoris Laetitia*, #264).

Always Echoing the Faith

Perhaps you know someone like my friend, a longtime catechetical leader, whose home sings of her three loves: family, culture, and God. Every room speaks of the goodness of God. Like a heartbeat, each wall and corner echoes the joy of the Gospel. Some may call these knickknacks, but the small statues, cards, quotations, etc., are more than decorative. In my friend's home, literally every visible surface repeats our loving God's constant invitation to new life in the Spirit. Immersed in this message, she leaves home carrying the Word of God to others.

Summary: The Fruit of the Spirit Is Love

The fruit of the Spirit is love, joy, peace, patience, kindness, generosity, faithfulness, gentleness, and self-control. There is no law against such things. (Gal. 5:22–23)

Baptism is not magical. Catechesis begins at home, and faith grows by living it within the small community of family. Family was designed by God to reflect the interconnected, distinct, equal persons of the Holy Trinity. The fruit of the Spirit as listed in Galatians 5 describes what this looks like. No family is perfect, but families can be holy. A home is not a classroom or school in the physical sense, nor is faith formed using the same teaching methods as mathematics or science. It is vitally important for the local Church to resume the posture that "parents have the primary responsibility for their children's faith formation" (*CCC*, #2223).

A robust catechetical program cannot substitute for the faith lessons learned within the family, but it can be a supportive structure. Grandparents can be a major support as they tap into their faith to reinforce parents' efforts and/or stand in proxy for them in the matter of faith formation. Sometimes within the family, emotional wounds must be mended for faith to grow. It is not uncommon for individuals who were hurt through family dynamics to have difficulty accepting God as a loving Parent, or siblings as brothers and sisters of the heart.

Given the hustle and bustle of modern life, catechetical programs need to meet families where they are. This may require creativity and flexibility in terms of time, location, and format. Today, likely vehicles for the journey include gathering online and/or away from the parish building, engaging in service learning, and utilizing multimedia resources. Intergenerational (also called whole community or family catechesis) is a promising approach that can provide something many families want—planned opportunities to spend quality time growing in faith together.

For Reflection and Discussion

- As a young person, what representations of faith did you encounter in the homes of family and friends?
- Quietly reflect on people in your life who exemplified Christian discipleship. Where were you? What was your age? Remember the various settings: sitting around the table or family room, riding in the car, or walking together. Recall people in the classroom, at the workplace, on retreat, or in church. Try to capture in a word a characteristic of each person that reminds you of Jesus. Thank God for bringing these experiences to mind, and pray for that person.

Growing as a Catechetical Leader

How are you reinforcing the vision of the domestic church in the parish or catechetical setting? Meal times and in-the-car talks are built-in opportunities. For some families, making every effort to attend Mass together regularly may be a good starting point. In addition, families can learn to practice Sabbath in the Jewish sense—meaning scheduling uninterrupted time to rest and play together.

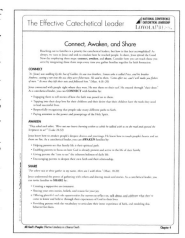

You probably have experienced or are familiar with several ways to help families celebrate the high liturgical seasons. How might you help them infuse faith into "secular" holidays as well? For example, how could families integrate faith practices when celebrating birthdays, while vacationing, on Memorial Day, or on Martin Luther King Jr.'s birthday? The spiritual practices do not have to be complicated, but commitment of the head of the household is imperative.

Go to www.loyolapress.com/ECL to access the worksheet.

Suggested Action

Reflect on your experiences in a sacred space within your home. Or create such a space that invites you to spend precious moments in conversation with God. Reflect on your experiences there as a model for the families you serve. Invite parents, grandparents, and godparents/sponsors to a session during which they discuss the idea of the domestic church. Ask members of the group to share memories or experiences in sacred areas of their homes. Resist the temptation to give a lecture or pass out a resource sheet on this subject. Rather, facilitate conversation that opens the door for visualizing holy spaces in their home and initiating or continuing family faith practices. Where in the home could space be dedicated to prayer? How would the environment look? Who would spend time there? Could members of the family use it for individual prayer or to gather at regular times?

For Further Consideration

Amoris Laetitia: The Joy of Love. Pope Francis (Frederick, MD: The Word Among Us, 2016).

The Great Emergence: How Christianity Is Changing and Why. Phyllis Tickle (Grand Rapids: Baker Books, 2008, 2012).

Raising Faith-Filled Kids: Ordinary Opportunities to Nurture Spirituality at Home. Tom McGrath (Chicago: Loyola Press, 2000).

Reimagining Faith Formation for the 21st Century: Engaging All Ages and Generations. John Roberto (Naugatuck, CT: Lifelong Faith Associates, 2015).

The Skilled Helper: A Problem-Management and Opportunity-Development Approach to Helping. Gerard Egan (Belmont, CA: Brooks/Cole, 2013).

Will There Be Faith? A New Vision for Educating and Growing Disciples. Thomas H. Groome (New York: HarperOne, 2011).

5
Faith for Grown-Ups: Adult Catechesis

Honey, You'll Be an Adult All Too Soon

"Wait until you are older . . ." or "When I grow up . . ." Parent-child exchanges like these have been happening for generations. There are children who can hardly wait to grow up and others who secretly follow Peter Pan's footprints. Some youth seem to glide into adulthood, while others arrive with a rough landing. No matter how we get there, adulthood remains an important season for continuing to nurture our faith.

In his book *Reimagining Faith Formation for the 21st Century: Engaging All Ages and Generations*, John Roberto describes adulthood as comprising five generations. He makes the case that effective faith formation will plan for ten decades of human life and provides detailed recommendations for how to accomplish this. Roberto emphasizes that there is no one-size-fits-all approach. After all, adult faith formation will achieve the desired outcome only if it responds to the evolving needs of transitioning, often overextended people in the twenty- to ninety-year age ranges.

Adulthood may be examined and understood as a long journey into the horizon that is punctuated by major intersections and unanticipated detours. At each stage of the journey—early adulthood, midlife, the mature years, and the senior years—distinct physical, cognitive, emotional, and spiritual markers emerge. Prepare to use the turn signal, if needed, because each juncture presents new opportunities and challenges for spiritual development. We will examine the first stage of early adulthood in chapter 6. Let's focus now on persons who have deeper roots in the land of grown-ups.

Three Snapshots of Adulthood

Midlife—Forget Cruise Control

Adults in their forties and fifties have achieved some personal and professional accomplishments. By this time, friends, acquaintances, and loved ones have died, and many have faced their own serious health concerns. Midlifers realize there is more to do with their lives, but they also may consider themselves to be halfway through life. This fact stimulates self-assessment and course adjustments. Adults in their forties to midfifties evaluate their significant relationships, work life, health, finances, mistakes, and unrealized dreams. The questions of identity and purpose now hinge on their relationships with others. As a consequence, they direct considerable attention toward leaving a legacy and generativity, which is the opposite of stagnation. They wonder, *What is the meaning of my life? What memory of my contributions and sacrifices will continue after I am gone?*

For many midlifers, the next step takes the shape of greater leadership or responsibility as administrators, consultants, and mentors. Cognitively, they are more skilled at reconciling differences and perceiving a situation from multiple vantage points. Thus, they are compelled at varying degrees to engage in deeper learning and soul searching. They increasingly care for others: many have become the safety net for aged parents, grown children, and/or grandchildren. At the same time, the quality of life after retirement is a major concern.

Spiritually, this turn in the road leads some midlife adults to contemplative prayer, self-examination, and a willingness to enter more fully into the mysteries of faith.

The Mature Years—or Sixty Is the New . . .

In the decades of the sixties and seventies, adults reach a level of emotional, intellectual, and physical development that can be labeled "mature." But don't label them old! These adults still want to exercise their independence, maintain good health, and enjoy both companionship and intimacy.

They attempt to use resources wisely. The self-awareness they have attained through various life lessons turns up the desire to enrich their lives with activities and people that bring joy and contentment. For instance, they may carve out time to be in nature, pursue hobbies, and/or spend quality time with others.

Seniors—Our Wise Elders

Adults over seventy-five years of age are a rapidly growing group as people live longer. This age group is nearly double that of the number of teenagers in the United States, cites Janet Schaeffler in *Seasons of Adult Faith Formation* (Lifelong Faith Associates, 2015). Many organizations, such as AARP (formerly the American Association of Retired Persons), have done much to uplift the dignity and image of seniors.

I prefer to use the term *elder* for this age group—a cultural term that connotes wisdom. Society derives intangible benefits from the presence of elders. Likewise, elders thrive when connected with others in various forms of community. Intergenerational catechesis enables members of the community to grow differently, yet together. Tapping into this interdependency has the potential to fortify families, the Church, and society.

At this stage of life, several physical changes are obvious. Dorothy Linthicum, a contributing writer to the book *Seasons of Adult Faith Formation*, observes that seniors are well aware of personal losses: death of a spouse, loss of hearing and eyesight, the wearing out of joints, and fading memory. Family responsibilities have likely diminished, but a senior's "bucket list" of things to do may not be exhausted. New questions arise: *My spirit may be willing, but can my body handle it? Is forgetfulness a lapse in memory or a sign of dementia?* Frequent hints of vulnerability begin to surface: take care not to fall, avoid fatigue, remember to take medications and pay bills. They may not receive as many hugs as children do, but they still cherish closeness and affection of others.

People in their eighties are looking across the street toward the afterlife, even more so than a few years earlier. Those who have experienced a long-term active faith life tend to seek more spiritual development. Some report that they pray more often, taking their concerns to God, anticipating a response of good counsel and anticipating comfort. Research also indicates that seniors who were detached from God earlier in life are less likely to turn to the Church for direction. Even so, the saying about old dogs and new tricks does not apply to humans.

Adult Learning Principles and Approaches

It's important for us as catechetical leaders to be aware of how adults learn. For adults to learn effectively, the following principles need to be respected:

- Adults are self-motivated—they resist having ideas imposed upon them.
- Adults bring life experience that must be respected.
- Adults are goal-oriented—they learn in order to cope with life transitions and want to apply what they learn immediately.

- Adults demand relevance and practicality, and they need to take ownership.
- Adults' time commitments must be respected.
- Adults learn best in relational, interactive, conversational settings.
- Adults like to laugh!

Adult faith formation is most effective when it takes on many different shapes and genres, so to speak, and avoids looking or feeling like going back to school. As you plan adult faith-formation opportunities, consider a variety of options, including local pilgrimages, book discussion groups, mentoring relationships, small faith-sharing groups, online learning initiatives, a YouTube channel of quality faith-formation videos, catechesis at existing parish meetings, service opportunities, and more.

Whatever you do, think outside the box, or at least outside the classroom. Don't rely solely on lectures, and get people talking to one another. Likewise, when it comes to adult faith formation, be sure that your offerings speak to people's everyday lives and needs. We have a habit of inviting adults to engage in topics that are very "churchy" instead of inviting them to get in touch with their hopes, dreams, joys, and struggles and to recognize God in the midst of them. In his book *A Church on the Move* (Loyola Press, 2016), Joe Paprocki offers the following list of "life" topics:

- celebrating life
- getting through difficult times
- letting go
- coping with change
- living heroically
- finding your source of energy
- developing deeper wisdom
- discovering courage
- reaching out to others
- living a more meaningful life

- coming to terms with suffering
- becoming a more loving person
- becoming a more selfless you
- learning from failure

Finally, reasons for gathering adults for faith formation need not always be "heavy." Consider gathering people to share faith around or connected to hobbies, such as walking, running, fishing, gardening, woodworking, painting, theater, camping, hiking, photography, cooking, and more. There's no rule that says adult faith formation needs to be so formal. Gathering around fun topics and hobbies can serve as an excellent form of pre-evangelization: a way of inviting people to get a flavor of the Catholic way of life without being intimidated by doctrine-heavy topics.

Dynamic Adult Faith Formation Exists!

Have you been to a catechetical conference or another promotion of parish programs lately? If so, you may have noticed a strong propensity for catechetical programs for youth—not so much for adults. But if we search in less visible places, we will find "unconventional" adult catechesis taking place. Groups gather regularly in coffee shops, in bars (Theology on Tap), and in homes to study the Bible or to learn what the Church teaches on a given subject.

There are abundant resources available in every conceivable format to help adults grow in spiritual maturity. These include a profusion of online materials, as well as hybrid physical/virtual learning networks. The magnitude of catechetical resources can be daunting without the assistance of knowledgeable "curators"—a term that John Roberto has made popular—who are skilled at identifying good material for particular needs. Often, those engaged in the learning process provide this assistance or complement it through personal recommendations and by sharing links to digital media that they find useful.

Why Concentrate on Adults Now?

There are countless examples of healthy youth catechetical programs. However, it is becoming more and more obvious that good youth catechesis does not guarantee well-formed adults. At the same time, research on generational religiosity indicates that effective adult catechesis increases the probability that youth will follow in those footsteps.

The catechetical formation of adults is essential for the Church to carry out Christ's commission to make disciples. This need is clearly addressed in the *National Directory for Catechesis*:

> The catechesis of adults . . . is the principal form of catechesis, because it is addressed to persons who have the greatest responsibilities and the capacity to live the Christian message in its fully developed form. . . . Because of its importance and because all other forms of catechesis are oriented in some way to it, the catechesis of adults must have high priority at all levels of the church. (*NDC*, #48A)

A fundamental challenge for catechetical leaders is to rethink how to facilitate spiritual maturity in adult disciples. Imparting knowledge is an important factor, but it is not the main course. Effectual adult catechesis will penetrate the mind, but its destiny is the heart.

Author Tom Zanzig advises that "those working in adult catechesis avoid the mistake of focusing far more on the transmission of content than on the transformation of persons" (*Seasons of Adult Faith Formation*). Likewise, in the words of Saint Paul, "Do not conform yourselves to this age but be transformed by the renewal of your mind, that you may discern what is the will of God, what is good and pleasing and perfect" (Rom. 12:2, NABRE). Faith formation should lead to heart *trans*formation!

Diversity in Faith: Catholic, Ecumenical, and Interreligious

Finally, we would be remiss in talking about adults without addressing the realities of ecumenism and interreligious dialogue. In today's complex families, people of different faiths often live under one roof. Unfortunately, there is a tendency to view the spectrum of diverse religious beliefs in light of popular social conditioning that warns, "Avoid discussing religion in public." Not only do misinformation and lack of tolerance for the religious beliefs of others further polarize us, they also create an obstacle to evangelization. With age and experience, adults grow in their ability to reconcile different perspectives, even opposites.

The Church teaches that God desires harmony and mutual respect among people of all creeds. A significant revelation from the Second Vatican Council was the Church's encouragement to engage in ecumenical and interreligious dialogue. Thomas Groome agrees:

> The challenge is not simply to learn about other religions. . . . We need religious education that enables people . . . to "cross over" into traditions other than their own with openness to learn from them for their own faith. This is when and where real understanding emerges, allowing us to move beyond toleration to appreciation of religious traditions that are truly "other" than "ours." (*Will There Be Faith?: A New Vision for Educating and Growing Disciples*, 80)

As with inculturation, this openness to understanding differences with mutual respect deepens rather than diminishes one's own spiritual development.

Our society reflects tremendous religious diversity. This plurality includes forces that misinterpret and disparage faith in any form. It is imperative that Christians know Jesus—not what others say about him, but that we *know Jesus for ourselves*. Likewise, it is important that those who profess to be Catholic know and understand authentic Church teaching and tradition. Advancing the mission of Christ depends on it! The key to harmony between people of different faiths is not to avoid talking about the subject but to engage in dialogue with an open mind and with a good, solid understanding of your own faith tradition.

Mission in the World: Catholic Social Teaching

As noted in chapter 3, the United States is an individualistic culture. Given that orientation and their countless material comforts, Americans swim in a culture that is competitive, materialistic, and increasingly secular. Christians in the land of plenty may be likened to the proverbial rich person trying to enter the Kingdom of God—it's easier for a camel to pass through the eye of a needle, Jesus said (see Luke 18:25). But effective adult catechesis can help those who wish to swim against the current that draws people toward spiritual death.

> Catechesis encourages an apprenticeship in Christian living that is based on Christ's teachings about community life. It should encourage a spirit of simplicity and humility, a special concern for the poor, particular care for the alienated, a sense of fraternal correction, common prayer, mutual forgiveness, and a fraternal love that embraces all these attitudes. Catechesis encourages the disciples of Christ to make their daily conduct a shining and convincing testimony to the Gospel. (*NDC*, #20.5)

Engaging adults in formation, activities, and experiences inspired by the principles of Catholic social teaching can be an effective way of transforming people's hearts and minds. For example, soliciting donations to maintain the parish food pantry is admirable. Yet, encountering families in need and working with local church or community organizations to address the source of hunger in the region touches the hearts of those giving and those receiving assistance. The principles of Catholic social teaching are

- **Dignity of the Human Person**—We are called to ask whether our actions as a society respect or threaten the life and dignity of the human person.

- **Call to Family, Community, and Participation**—We are called to support the family (the principle social institution) so that people can participate in society, build a community spirit, and promote the well-being of all.

- **Rights and Responsibilities**—We are called to protect the rights that all people have to those things required for a decent human life, such as food, clothing, and shelter.

- **Option for the Poor and Vulnerable**—We are called to pay special attention to the needs of those who are poor.

- **Dignity of Work and the Rights of Workers**—We are called to protect the basic rights of all workers: the right to engage in productive work, fair wages, and private property and the right to organize, join unions, and pursue economic opportunity.

- **Solidarity**—We are called to recognize that because God is our Father, we are all brothers and sisters, with the responsibility to care for one another.

- **Care for God's Creation**—We are called to care for all that God has made.

Catechesis in a Different Location

If catechesis is about continuous formation of disciples in Jesus Christ, where does one begin with adults? What is necessary, relevant, and desirable for adults with many simultaneous roles and responsibilities? What are the spiritual needs of parents and caregivers, of citizens, of students, of the unemployed and underemployed? How might artists, advocates, mentors, coaches, and business leaders benefit from an active prayer life and intimate relationship with God?

As a catechetical leader, take time to assess the opportunities for ongoing, integrated spiritual growth in your parish or program. Do existing programs and structures meet the needs of parents, grandparents, engaged couples, widows, and widowers? Are there offerings that attract empty nesters and adults with no children? Is there anything that appeals to the spiritual interests of those who are busy and of those who have extra time? Formation does not happen always or best through a course of study. Participating in service and outreach efforts, parish ministries, small-group discussions, retreats, lectures, and pilgrimages are some of the avenues that can lead adults to a deeper encounter with the divine.

Adults tend to know what they want to learn and the methods that work for them. Often, older adults prefer face-to-face communications, while young adults function quite well working online in their pajamas. Theological reflection will appeal to some adults and not others. Some individuals will make a faith connection through learning about issues affecting the community and developing responses in light of the gospel and Catholic social teaching. Many adults want to know how to pray.

In *Reimagining Faith Formation for the 21st Century*, John Roberto points out that catechesis takes place in a different location now. It has moved from educational institutions to networks, from classrooms to a variety of physical places and virtual spaces, available at any time of day. He states that the major workings and basic expectations of catechesis have been adjusted "from consumption to participatory learning."

These are more than cosmetic adjustments. They are radical (root) changes, brought about by a quiet revolution while our sights were fixed in the opposite direction—the past. The effective catechetical leader is recalibrating to meet these needs and expectations.

Following Jesus' Lead

Technology has changed, but the message of the gospel is changeless. To understand the "new" roles in the learning enterprise, study the teaching approach that Jesus took. Here is an example from the Gospel of John.

On an ordinary day, while approaching Samaria, Jesus chose a different route. Instead of going around the forbidden zone, Jesus entered the town. There, he met a woman who opened herself to a personal and life-changing encounter with the Messiah. They did not hurry the conversation; neither did they waste time with idle talk. Jesus stepped over several barriers of cultural bias—gender, ethnicity, religion. He persistently turned the theological discussion to her concerns and needs. Speaking with authority and love, Jesus guided the Samaritan woman to a new self-awareness. So meaningful was this encounter that many came to believe in the One sent by the Father. (See John 4:4–42.)

How amazing would parishes and communities be if adult disciples opened themselves to continuous conversation with the Lord! In his book *Will There Be Faith? A New Vision for Educating and Growing Disciples,* Thomas Groome summarizes Jesus' pedagogy (teaching style):

- Begin with people's lives. (Jesus looked at the woman's current reality.)
- Encourage their own reflections. (Jesus asked her to think about her life in a whole new way.)
- Teach the gospel with authority. (Jesus spoke with integrity, from God, as the source of truth.)
- Invite them to see Jesus for themselves. (Jesus helped the woman see who he really was.)

- Encourage them to live out their faith as disciples. (Jesus gave her a new life, and she wanted to share it with others.)

Summary: Lord, Give Us This Living Water

Jesus answered and said to her, "Everyone who drinks this water will be thirsty again; but whoever drinks the water I shall give will never thirst; the water I shall give will become in him a spring of water welling up to eternal life." The woman said to him, "Sir, give me this water, so that I may not be thirsty and have to keep coming here to draw water." (John 4:13–15, NABRE)

The words that Jesus spoke to the Samaritan woman at the well are the same words he speaks to us now: "Whoever drinks the water I shall give will never thirst; the water I shall give will become in [them] a spring of water welling up to eternal life." For all our earnest efforts, the seed of faith grows not by our power and creativity but through the initiative of God by the power of the Holy Spirit. The heart of adult catechesis lies in these truths:

At the heart of all we are and do as the Church is a revelation of great Good News: God, who is love, has made us to enjoy divine life in abundance, to share in the very life of God, a communion with the Holy Trinity together with all the saints in the new creation of God's reign.

Faith, which is a gift from God, is our human response to this divine calling: It is a personal adherence to God and assent to his truth. Through searching and growth, conversion of mind and heart, repentance and reform of life, we are led by God to turn from the blindness of sin and to accept God's saving grace, liberating truth, and sustaining love for our lives and for all of creation. (*Our Hearts Were Burning within Us*, USCCB, 1999)

For Reflection and Discussion

- With your catechetical team, discuss the adjustments you have made in your approach to adult catechetical ministry in the past five years. In your reflection, consider three aspects:

  ○ How you think about the work/ministry to adults

  ○ Your teaching methods

  ○ Your expectations of those to be catechized

- Ask each person to draw a sketch of him- or herself in a catechetical setting three to five years ago, and then draw another sketch of themselves today in catechetical training. Compare the two drawings. Identify any substantive changes.

Growing as a Catechetical Leader

Are you a young adult, middle-aged, mature, or a senior? Based on your birth year, what is your cohort: Baby Boomer, Generation X, Millennial, or Builder Generation? Do you relate to that moniker or not? Besides all that, how old do you feel?

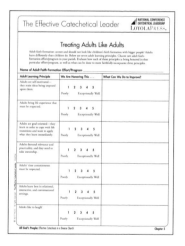

As with physical maturation, spiritual development ebbs and flows, sometimes flourishing, at other times appearing dormant. The four-seasons-of-life metaphor only partially captures the transitions experienced in adulthood. The way each person moves through the seasons is influenced by many factors—the generation, culture, family relations, the "stuff" that just happens on the journey—and all these shape one's outlook and response to God's offer of abundant life.

Awareness of one's current position on the journey has the potential to generate new empathy for the challenges that other adults are facing today. Where are you on the adulthood spectrum? How would you describe the season you are in today? Are you growing spiritually, or is your spirit hibernating at this time? What is the evidence of either growth or dormancy? What particular spiritual practices or forms of prayer is God utilizing in this season to draw you closer?

Go to www.loyolapress.com/ECL to access the worksheet.

Suggested Action

Note specific ways that adult catechesis can prepare Catholics to live in community and to participate actively in the life and mission of the Church. How might your current effective adult-catechetical program be adjusted to generate more coworkers in God's vineyard, who will cultivate an active commitment to service, justice, care for creation, peace building, and all aspects of promoting a culture of life?

For Further Consideration

Concise Guide to Adult Faith. Neil Parent (Notre Dame, IN: Ave Maria Press, 2009).

Our Hearts Were Burning within Us (Washington, DC: United States Conference of Catholic Bishops, 1999).

Reimagining Faith for the 21st Century: Engaging All Ages and Generations. John Roberto (Naugatuck, CT: Lifelong Faith Associates, 2015).

Seasons of Adult Faith Formation. John Roberto, ed. (Naugatuck, CT: Lifelong Faith Associates, 2015).

Toward an Adult Church: A Vision of Faith Formation. Jane Regan (Chicago: Loyola Press, 2002).

Will There Be Faith? A New Vision for Educating and Growing Disciples. Thomas H. Groome (New York: HarperOne, 2011).

United States Catholic Catechism for Adults (U.S. Conference of Catholic Bishops, 2006).

6

Young, Not Youth: Catechesis and Young Adults

When Is PB&J Not PB&J?

Youth and young adults are almost always linked in the language of pastoral ministry. Like cats and dogs, these two groups are often spoken of in the same breath, but they definitely have different identities. On a discussion thread on social media, one pastoral minister lamented, "Is it just me, or are a lot of people in ministry still working out of a mind-set that young adults are just teens who have graduated from high school?" When planning for catechesis with young adults, try to visualize "peanut butter and jelly" in a form other than a sandwich.

Young adulthood is a period of tremendous change, marked by a strong awareness of being in transition. Emerging adults feel the dual pulls of intimacy and isolation, of cooperation and competition, of being young yet no longer a youth (in the U.S. context). The late teens (emerging adulthood), twenties, and thirties are a time of hope and possibilities, of emotional highs and lows. Young adults are entrenched in evaluating the contents of their life. At this stage, much social capital is directed toward determining which behaviors and beliefs to retain and which ones to release. Given their new freedom and responsibility, young adults begin test-driving various roads in search of significant relationships, satisfying work, and mature spiritual identity.

The bishops' pastoral plan for ministry with young adults, *Sons and Daughters of the Light* (USCCB, 1996), underscores four commonly recognized focus areas of young adults:

- personal identity
- relationships
- work
- spiritual life

In addition, the document points out that these focus areas "are undertaken over an extended period of time, for some, into their thirties; and there is a lack of family, civic, and pastoral institutions to support them." These are just some of the reasons young adulthood is perhaps the most challenging period for catechetical formation.

One factor that unites young adults with other young people well into their twenties is the continued development of the frontal cortex of the brain. This region regulates emotions, impulses, and abstract thinking. Thus, as they mature, young adults gain capacity for executive functions, e.g., navigating risks, making sound judgments, and assessing their own and other perspectives. It has been said that this is the time of orienting the map toward "true north" before taking off.

From Taxiing to Takeoff

By the time emerging adults enter their thirties, many feel more confident. At this point, they leave the tarmac and begin to ascend! They are growing into a better sense of personal identity, settling into work and career, and further establishing their credentials. Some make a home for themselves and/or create their own family. Social scientist Donald Capps describes this as the "decade of competence" (Kyle Oliver, "Young Adulthood," in *Seasons of Adult Faith Formation*).

Then, there are thirty-somethings who take off from the tarmac but find themselves working through the devastating experience of divorce or the end of an intimate relationship that did not lead to marriage. Today, growing segments of young adults have difficulty securing and sustaining work that affords independent living. Current data reveal rising numbers of young adults returning home until they can get on their feet again. Referred to as "the boomerang effect," this decision to move home results from a variety of factors. Some are the consequences of personal decisions; other factors are beyond the individual's control.

Periods of crisis are precipitated by loss of employment, divorce, addiction, single parenthood, and casualties of military service. These circumstances drive many people to seek restoration and healing through an established program or a welcoming, supportive community. At this point, involvement in a church appeals to many emerging adults. An invitation to hear from an expert on the problem with an opportunity for interaction—either in person or online—may catch the attention of a troubled young adult. Effective catechetical programs need to offer attractive options that address these difficult situations, at times and in locations that accommodate the needs of young adults.

Women- or Men-Only Groups

Some researchers further distinguish the development paths of males and females. For example, women are wired to be more concerned with relationship identity; men are more directed toward work identity (Kyle Oliver, "Young Adulthood," in *Seasons of Adult Faith Formation*). This distinction may be the effect of women hearing the biological clock ticking as men watch the professional time clock.

This is not to imply that women do not attend to their professional development, or men to building satisfying relationships. But the difference in emphasis and urgency bears consideration when planning adult catechetical programs. Faith-sharing groups just for women or just for men offer an environment that may be more responsive to the spiritual formation of young adults. Like the experience of attending a single-gender high school or college, such prayer and study groups encourage a freedom of self-exploration that transcends the individual's image as he or she perceives it is reflected in the eyes of the opposite gender.

Diversity Really Is a Thing

Cultural diversity was discussed in earlier chapters but warrants another look—particularly regarding our catechetical ministry to young adults. Generally, young adults today have had more exposure to other cultural and language groups than have their predecessors. Integrated schools and clubs, semesters abroad and mission trips, and popular media allow them many opportunities to view "the other."

However, without authentic personal encounters, young adults will be ill-prepared for healthy relationships across cultures. Superficial observation does little to remove barriers that are sustained through stereotypes, generational prejudice, and lack of knowledge. Campus ministers and military chaplains can play a significant role in the lives of young adults living away from home, who often encounter more diversity than in their hometown. Consequently, it is of major importance for young-adult ministry leaders to develop intercultural competence. Yet, too often, campus ministry offices at colleges and universities do not seem welcoming or do not adequately address the spiritual needs of diverse students and staff.

For example, many operate out of a common assumption that Hispanic students are Catholic and African Americans are not. Consider the missed evangelization opportunities caused by such presumptions.

The campus ministry door may be open to everyone, but does it offer programs or resources that are culturally responsive?

$ = Blessing + Curse

Many young adults struggle with financial independence. Young people are increasingly burdened with college debt and employment that doesn't provide health insurance or vacation benefits. Yet popular culture glamorizes material comforts and may promote a false sense of entitlement. At times, this generates stress and discontent in individuals who want to reconcile their finances with their beliefs and values. They have tough choices to make.

Many young adults aspire to ease suffering in the world. They are troubled by the widening economic and opportunity gaps between communities. As some young adults experience growing prosperity, others battle pervasive poverty. This disparity also exists regarding availability of parish/diocesan ministry resources. However, the message of Catholic teaching and tradition is consistent: "Both the disadvantaged and the affluent must come to know through catechesis that the ultimate goal of the Christian life is communion with God, not power, riches, and influence" (*NDC*, #4C).

The passion that young adults have for economic justice can serve as an entry point for your faith-formation efforts targeting this age group. In other words, leading with an invitation to explore doctrinal concepts will not be as effective as leading with an invitation to participate in works of mercy and social action.

Tech Savvy

Let's face it: the contemporary lifestyle is organized by and through ever-changing devices, systems, and gadgets of technology. Mobile devices, social media, and online networks have an impact on nearly every aspect of a young adult's daily life. Swiping and clicking are essential conduits for working, learning, relaxing, and cultivating relationships. As automobiles, television, and indoor utilities affected the way of life for previous generations, today's digital technology influences behavior and thought processes in more profound ways than just their labor-saving properties. (Think, for example, of how you were affected when you last left your cell phone at home. Other than annoyance, did you perceive a spiritual reaction?)

Today's young adults have grown up with increasingly sophisticated digital technology. Thus, catechizing young adults must incorporate technology as the vehicle, not the destination. Just as a live performance is experienced differently from a recorded broadcast, there is no substitute for face-to-face interaction. Technology facilitates the teaching/learning process in fundamental ways. But God made us to live *in community*, not in isolation. People desire personal relationships even when they seem elusive.

Young adults report feeling alone in a crowd. By contrast, the Holy Spirit gathers Jesus' disciples together in love and solidarity. Effective catechesis leads those searching for community deeper into the life of the Holy Trinity to fulfill the will of God. As the Church teaches, "The ultimate end of the whole divine economy is the entry of God's creatures into the perfect unity of the Blessed Trinity" (*CCC*, #260).

Intimate Relationships and Questioning

When emerging young adults choose to further their education, enter the workforce, relocate, marry, or profess a religious life, many are introduced to different faiths, cultures, values, and practices. Adolescent friendships may change or fade. Tensions surface as young adults attempt to negotiate the values of contemporary society and those of their family. This may be heightened in immigrant families that seek to balance their heritage and traditional cultural values against contemporary American social mores. The present generation of young adults has been tagged "the first truly multicultural and multimedia generation" (M. Carolyn Clark, *Handbook of Young Adult Religious Education*, 214–215).

The big elephant in the room for young adults is sexuality. Our social environment is hypersexualized through visual media, music, the Internet, etc. Sexual messages saturate print, broadcast, and digital advertisements, entertainment, and prime-time television and radio programming. On the surface, it appears that the simple bottom line is that culture says yes and the Church says no. Young adults want to know why. Spiritually, young adults yearn for truth, purpose, intimacy, and fulfillment. Where can they find deep satisfaction? The answers they seek are not found in sexual exploits, excessive shopping, alcohol, drugs, or partying.

Young adults are very self-focused, trying on different identities in search of their authentic selves. "Some experience this searching as a quiet inner questioning—a thoughtful reexamination of traditional beliefs. Others accomplish this by learning more about their faith. For still others, this searching can lead to a functional atheism, a rejection of organized religion, or a distancing from church activities and worship" (*Sons and Daughters of the Light*, USCCB, 1996).

A Picture of Young Faith

In addition to the four Gospels, the Acts of the Apostles tells the Christian story in a manner that many people more easily relate to than the figures and events of the Old Testament. While the New Testament continues the story of God's salvation and love for us, the Book of Acts particularly recounts stories of evangelization. It paints a picture of a young faith that is tested and deepening. It shows us new disciples (apprentices) attempting to follow The Way of Jesus Christ, to hasten the reign of God. The Book of Acts can be considered an introduction to the story of current and future disciples.

Young adults want to hear the truth of the gospel conveyed with authority and love. The liturgy is one place where this can happen for those who actively participate in the life of the Church. Researchers have learned that young adults want quality worship that is well prepared. This includes good music and a meaningful message that is well delivered. Many crave opportunities for prayerful contemplation, such as in Eucharistic adoration, Taizé prayer, or Rosary recitation. Others find charismatic prayer and spirited music to be healing and compelling. Young adults, grappling for the meaning of faith and its expression in their lives, are attracted by sincerity in those who profess the faith. Do they see love in action and feel accepted? How are others like themselves regarded by members of the faith community? They are watching the behavior of Catholic Christians in public places, as well. Criticism, gossip, pride, and hypocrisy thwart many good intentions. Perfunctory worship also can obstruct the movement of the Holy Spirit.

Sacramental Living: More Than a Moment

For many Catholics, sacramental life is an unopened gift in plain sight. Catechetical leaders can utilize sacramental preparation as formation for young adults, furthering the likelihood that these moments will yield more than cherished memorabilia. Faith can be awakened in young adults when they prepare for the sacraments of initiation, matrimony, or baptism of their child. Direct participation in the sacraments can be a contemporary experience of mystagogy, a timely, gentle invitation to enter the sacred mysteries of faith.

Likewise, the young adult who serves as a godparent in baptism or sponsors a confirmation candidate encounters a catechetical moment. What is understood about the purpose of the sacrament? How is this responsibility perceived? Visiting the sick may open another portal to active faith when the young adult is present during a chaplain's visit or observes a priest anointing his or her gravely ill relative or friend.

Jesus sent out the disciples to minister in pairs. In the same way, one who is searching spiritually may be encouraged to go deeper into the spiritual realm when accompanying a friend who brings the Eucharist to a shut-in. Well-formed faith is meant to be shared. Adult catechesis forms leaders who delight in sharing the "joy of the gospel."

Key to Developing Mature Faith

Thomas Groome's "Life to Faith to Life" pedagogy is particularly relevant for young-adult catechesis. This framework examines life in the light of faith and applies what is revealed in faith to the issues and circumstances of one's life. Groome speaks of access to Christian story and vision so that it resonates and connects in meaningful ways with the actual lives of people. Faith matures in young adults in a natural way when they are part of a supportive community of others like themselves, examining real-life concerns together through the lens of faith.

Optimism, vitality, enthusiasm; being idealistic, adventure-seeking, and on the cutting-edge—these qualities endear young adults to older and younger generations. Likewise, the same characteristics can animate evangelization and ministry efforts in the Church and society. This doesn't happen accidentally, though. Parishes must consciously, proactively, and intentionally invite and welcome young adults to partake in the liturgical and community life of the Church.

Sadly, many young adults are turned off by the dissonance between the Church as it is and the Church as it is called to be. Some display cynicism, distrust, and boredom with social institutions, including the Church. As the Church observed during the Second Vatican Council, "This split between the faith which many [Christians] profess and their daily lives deserves to be counted among the more serious errors of our age" (*Gaudium et Spes: Pastoral Constitution on the Church in the Modern World*, #43). Perhaps you, too, have heard horror stories of young adults offering their time and talent, only to be refused, discouraged, or ignored. Too often, older parishioners are uncomfortable relinquishing the reins of leadership or think themselves too busy to mentor new ministry members. Unfortunately, some pillars of the Church are resistant to new ideas. Have they forgotten that by today's standard, Jesus was a young adult?

At one time, a popular slogan in the U.S. was, "Don't trust anyone over thirty!" Nowadays, some of the older generation seem to avoid contact with young adults. It is time to bridge the gap. Prepare to leave the comfort zone. Initiate conversations with young adults. Facilitate life and faith conversations in settings other than the church, if possible.

Catholic Teaching and Politics

Modern-day disciples are gravely concerned about the effects of public policy on vulnerable persons and communities, the influence of media on character development, the sustainability of our environment, etc. All these matters demand a nonpartisan, moral response. Then add to our limited time, energy, and finances our work or study, caring for family members, monitoring our health, guarding the safety of our families, pursuing dreams, participating in associations, and keeping up with social media. When does one have time to pray or develop spiritually?

Particularly in the United States, religion has become a private matter—we keep our beliefs to ourselves so as not to offend or be offended. This disposition actually is at odds with the divine goal of discipleship and has become somewhat grafted to partisan politics. Consequently, many good church folk feel more polarized and conflicted than informed and empowered to live as public witnesses. They tend to distance themselves from unpopular positions.

The shorthand labels—conservative or progressive, red or blue states, life or dignity—bind us to categories that do not fully describe who we are. Instead of labels, the magisterium directs us to a path of love in action. Catholic social teaching helps us embrace a consistent life ethic and utilize the mirror of faith to assess a wide range of issues and determine our responses accordingly.

Implications for Young-Adult Faith Formation

The overall goals of young-adult faith formation, as articulated by the U.S. bishops in *Sons and Daughters of the Light*, are to connect young adults with

1. Jesus Christ
2. the Church, by inviting and welcoming their presence in the Christian community
3. the mission of the Church in the world
4. a peer community in which their faith is nurtured and strengthened

With these goals in mind, and considering the unique needs, hopes, desires, gifts, and challenges of today's young adults, let's explore some important implications for planning and executing faith formation for young adults.

- **Listen.** Don't do anything before you *listen* to young adults! The first and biggest mistake you can make is to create a plan in a vacuum without tapping into the expressed needs and wants of young adults. Gather a group of young adults together for a listening session, and then use that as a catalyst for formulating faith-formation opportunities.

- **Engage.** Avoid the temptation to be the "provider" of faith formation for young adults, who place a very high value on participation and interaction. The maxim "If you build it, they will come" does not apply, because young adults want to be cocreators and partners in things they are involved in. At every step of the way, be sure to involve young adults in the shaping of their own faith formation. Let the following guide your approach: "If *they* build it, they will come!"

- **Think digital.** For young adults, their mobile device is a primary way of connecting with the world. They do not draw a line of distinction between the digital and the physical worlds but rather view them seamlessly. Be sure to consider how you will communicate digitally with young adults, not only as a form of inviting but also as a form of delivering content, while not replacing face-to-face encounters. The digital world exists to enhance communication between human beings, much like a microphone enhances but does not replace a speaker's voice. Digital faith-formation experiences should always culminate in face-to-face encounters.

- **Rely on relationships, not gimmicks.** Young adults can sniff out phoniness in an instant, and they are not impressed with gimmicky approaches. Rather, they value authenticity and relationships. As you plan and execute faith formation for young adults, a key factor for your success will be the extent to which you forge relationships with young adults.

- **Offer adventure.** Young adults seek adventure and challenge and are eager to participate in experiences. Rather than offer courses, seminars, or classes for young-adult faith formation, consider offerings that invite young adults to an experience that includes a sense of challenge and adventure. For example, kick off Lent with an "Ash Wednesday Run/Walk to Fight Hunger." Invite young adults to run or walk a 5K or 10K course that culminates in receiving Lenten ashes on their foreheads at the finish line. You can follow this with a brief presentation on the Lenten disciplines and how young adults can participate in fighting hunger during Lent.

- **Tap their expertise.** Social media has permitted young adults to share their own expertise (or at least their opinions) on any number of topics and issues. As a result, they are comfortable turning to nontraditional "experts" for insight and guidance. Use this to your advantage by inviting young adults to be speakers and responders at faith-formation experiences. For example, going back to the Ash Wednesday suggestion above, the brief presentation following the run/walk can certainly include input from the pastor or someone on the pastoral staff such as yourself, but it can also include a panel of young adults invited to share how they plan to observe Lent and practice its disciplines. Even when you bring in an "expert" speaker on a topic, arrange for one or two young adults to serve as responders who share their impressions of what they just heard as well as their own insights. Because of social media, young adults are accustomed to adding their voices to anything that is being discussed.

- **Don't isolate them.** Young adults do not want to be treated differently but want to be recognized as "having arrived." While it can be helpful to gather young adults for experiences tailored specifically for their age group, avoid isolating them as a separate grouping in the parish. Young adults seek to be mentored by older adults and wish for their own voices to be heard by the same. Think intergenerational, but be sure to enable and empower young adults to take the lead instead of relying on the "usual suspects," who are most often middle-aged parishioners.

- **Think viral.** Young adults are accustomed to things "going viral" in the world of social media. In his book *Contagious: Why Things Catch On*, author Jonah Berger cites seven reasons why things go viral. Keep the following list in mind as you plan faith-formation experiences for young adults:

1. **Create experiences that reflect well on participants.** Young adults value the opportunity to be privy to helpful and insightful information that they can share with others, thus enabling themselves to be seen as intelligent, cutting-edge, well-informed, and relevant. Faith-formation experiences for young adults should offer them insights and information that is helpful for daily living and that they will be eager to share with others.

2. **Tap into what's on people's minds.** Saint Ignatius of Loyola advocated an approach to winning people over by "entering through their door but being sure to leave through your door." In other words, he recommended tapping into what is on people's minds already—their lived experience—helping them to see how God is intimately involved in their everyday lives.

3. **Provoke emotion.** Effective faith formation always needs to aim at both the head and the heart. Young adults are eager to see and feel authentic human affect and compassion in a world that is often so cold and unfeeling. Berger reminds us that "when we care, we share." Faith formation for young adults should tap into and provoke emotions that will drive them to action.

4. **Offer something that can be seen.** Young adults seek input and advice from their peers and are highly influenced by their peers' likes and dislikes. Faith-formation experiences for young adults should be something worthy of posting so that other young adults might see that their peers are finding value in your parish's offerings.

5. **Offer something practical.** Too often, young adults view Church teaching as too ethereal to have any relation to everyday life, primarily because we as a Church have tended to present it in such a manner. Faith formation for young adults needs to be practical and relatable to everyday living. In other words, avoid "churchy" language in your "packaging" of young-adult faith-formation opportunities.

6. **Encourage storytelling.** Storytelling is at the heart of the Judeo-Christian experience. Faith formation is not a vehicle for explaining the mystery of faith but rather for inviting people to enter into the mystery of faith. Storytelling is a portal to the world of mystery. Young-adult faith formation should encourage participants to both hear and share stories of faith, in order to recognize how our individual stories are tied to *the* story of salvation in and through Jesus Christ.

7. **Focus outward.** Finally, young adults are eager to make a positive impact on the world, so be sure to imbue your young-adult faith-formation opportunities with an outward focus. Include personal growth, but also talk about how our faith can positively affect and even change the world. Follow the advice of Dorothy Day, who insisted that everything a baptized person does should be, directly or indirectly, related to the corporal and spiritual works of mercy. Unlike some who reduce Christianity to a philosophy, Dorothy Day knew that Christianity is an embodied set of practices: things that we *do* for others. In his book *The Strangest Way* (Orbis Books, 2002), Bishop Robert Barron tells us that the works of mercy "compel a self-regarding ego outward in the direction of mission and connection, and, as such, they constitute a distinctively Christian social theory, radically out of step with modern social arrangements" (152). This type of thinking resonates with today's young adults.

There is a certain urgency about young-adult faith formation. These are new parents, future caretakers of the elderly, and trendsetters. This group of citizens will establish public policy, decide whether the country goes to war and how to spend public funds. They are the promising professionals that corporations recruit, the emerging scientists discovering life-saving treatments, the educators of our youth. They are the clergy we prayed God would send. Faith formation should help young adults meet Jesus, show them how to pray, and assist with forming conscience.

The direct approach is well described by Thomas Groome's "Faith to Life to Faith" teaching technique, discussed above. Using this method, catechesis will rekindle childhood faith exploration for some young adults and will introduce exciting and perhaps unsettling new experiences to others. Two nonnegotiable priorities for catechetical leaders accompanying young adults are to (1) find innovative ways to invite and engage young adults and (2) form and mentor new leaders.

Summary: The Lord Added to Their Number

They devoted themselves to the teaching of the apostles and to the communal life, to the breaking of the bread and to the prayers. . . . And every day the Lord added to their number those who were being saved. (Acts 2:42, 47, NABRE)

Catechizing young adults today requires swimming against very strong currents. Their point of reference for faith may be grandparents, if anyone at all. Furthermore, respect for religion is fading in the fabric of U.S. culture. Not only is the moral voice muted in the public space, but also almost any mention of religion is met with suspicion and ridicule. Humanism is trending globally today. There is a quiet push to pursue virtue without God.

Young adults are acclimated to easily integrate new technology in their lives. However, image makers with deep pockets dress progress as an ever-changing spectrum of options, freedom to choose, survival of the fittest, and so much fluff. Young people who have reached majority and sexual maturity, who now make their own financial decisions and lifestyle choices, will not accept a standardized, codified faith-formation curriculum. Instead, they will continue searching in places other than the Church for answers to essential life questions. Young adults seek the redemption that discipleship offers without necessarily realizing how they are being directed. It is not for us to know the ultimate outcome for individuals, but we know that God has already written the thrilling conclusion.

For Reflection and Discussion

- What are some of the most effective ways you have seen for reaching out to and connecting with young adults in the area of faith formation?

- What are the greatest needs of today's young adults? How can your parish meet these needs and challenges?

- What are your greatest obstacles to effective faith formation for young adults?

Growing as a Catechetical Leader

All disciples—young adults included—need to encounter Jesus in the faith community, in the Eucharist, and in service to others. As you offer your prayers and best efforts, be sure to convey a vital message to young adults. God continuously and with constant love beckons each of us to enter into the fullness of life with the Holy Trinity. For young adults, this invitation can be particularly meaningful as they exercise responsibility for newly acquired independence, particularly in matters of faith.

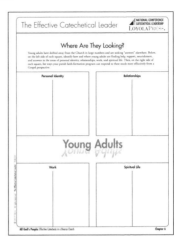

It appears Pope Francis doesn't miss an opportunity to encourage openness to encountering and accompanying one another, including those we may view as "other." (See *Evangelii Gaudium: The Joy of the Gospel.*) Both concepts are well suited to the faith formation of young adults. Encountering and accompanying young adults on the journey—in the flesh and in the spirit—demonstrates respect and extends love. This is how to meet them where they are.

Go to www.loyolapress.com/ECL to access the worksheet.

Suggested Action

Read about the disciples on the road to Emmaus in Luke 24:13–35. This story lays out Jesus' catechetical approach while instructing catechetical leaders on the process of conversion. Make a list of each step of Jesus' catechetical actions. After completing the list, review each action. Note whether you currently follow that action, and cite an example from your ministry experience. Also, identify any steps that you don't take. Ask God to show you how to incorporate those actions into your catechetical approach.

For Further Consideration

National Directory for Catechesis (Washington, DC: United States Conference of Catholic Bishops, 2005).

Seasons of Adult Faith Formation. John Roberto, ed. (Naugatuck, CT: Lifelong Faith Associates, 2015).

Sons and Daughters of the Light: A Pastoral Plan for Ministry with Young Adults (Washington, DC: United States Conference of Catholic Bishops, 2010).

Will There Be Faith? A New Vision for Educating and Growing Disciples. Thomas H. Groome (New York: HarperOne, 2011).

The National Study of Youth and Religion. Christian Smith and Lisa Pierce (University of Notre Dame, 2001—2010).

The Joy of Adolescent Catechesis (National Federation for Catholic Youth Ministry, National Catholic Education Association, National Conference for Catechetical Leadership, 2016).

7

The Young Church of Today: Adolescent Catechesis

"If Only I Knew Then What I Know Now. . . ."

In my experience, there is more tension in catechizing teens than any other age group. Even if one's adolescent years were full of fun, close friendships, and accolades, few of us who have made that journey would want to repeat it. Frankly, many adults, including some of us who minister to teens, still bear scars from junior high and senior high school days. We often look back thinking, "If only I knew then what I know now. . . ."

Adults who work with adolescents in the Church (excluding parents) tend to fall into one of two distinct roles: youth minister or catechetical leader. In many parishes, youth ministry and catechesis operate in separate orbits. Dedicated ministry leaders and well-meaning volunteers from both camps are passionate about bringing young people to Jesus Christ. Yet they steer their own vehicles in separate lanes and may take alternate routes in hopes of arriving at the same destination!

Some youth ministers relate exceptionally well with this age group yet shy away from formally teaching the faith out of fear that teens will see them as boring and lose interest. Meanwhile, many catechists who are committed to adolescent faith formation would be hard-pressed to chaperone a dance or a social outing with teenagers. Nevertheless, ministry with teenagers requires both skill sets, and there is a cross-training effect as youth interact regularly with adults in the Church.

When adults who are charged with youth ministry and adolescent catechesis approach their respective ministries in a way that disconnects faith formation from fun with peers, the adults and the youth they serve risk missing the big picture. Without discounting the different goals and activities in these ministry areas, the essential question for the Church is whether adult leaders, the pastoral team, parents, and other grown-ups in the pews are communicating a consistent message of the gospel of Jesus Christ in an engaging manner.

The Youthful Vision of the Pope

A signature mark of the long papacy of Saint John Paul II was his direct appeal to the Young Church. Before selfies with Pope Francis came into vogue, young adults and teens followed John Paul II on World Youth Day pilgrimages. An image of the Young Church as pilgrims searching for God emerged during his papacy. They studied his teachings in Catholic schools and embraced the Gospel of Life. The writings of John Paul II amplified his predecessors' words and reflected on the signs of the times in ways that brought social justice to the forefront, with new language and ideas, such as "solidarity" and "development."

Many were inspired by John Paul II's fluency in languages and the display of intercultural competency, which enabled him to speak with ease to much of the world. For instance, jazz vocalist Sarah Vaughan performed and recorded a series of John Paul II's early poetry, translated into English and set to music, which captured the universality of humanity yearning for divine fulfillment.

Because the pontiff recognized the Young Church in word and gesture, this generation glimpsed holiness in their lifetime. As a consequence, there was a bump in vocations and spiritual movements in the Church in the 1970s. Until recently, this was the only pope that Generation-X Catholics knew, and his direct appeal to youth was unprecedented. In 1976, the U.S. Conference of Catholic Bishops developed a *Vision of Youth Ministry,* followed by further study and the subsequent release of *Renewing the Vision: A Framework for Catholic Youth Ministry* (1997).

Evolution of Ministry with Adolescents

The new vision for teen faith formation articulated in these documents is a pronounced shift from the schoolhouse religious-education model on the one hand and the ski trip/theme park/pizza-and-gym night on the other. This framework tackles the spiritual development of teens comprehensively by "integrating ministry with adolescents and their families into the total life and mission of the Church" (*Renewing the Vision*). It acknowledges responsibility of the whole community, without relieving parents, catechetical leaders, and pastors of their canonical duties.

Renewing the Vision articulates three goals for ministry with adolescents:

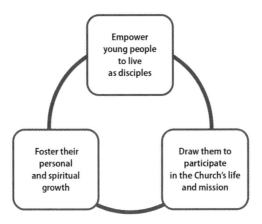

Specifically speaking to adolescent catechesis, the bishops explain: "Genuine faith is a total response of the whole person—mind, heart, and will. The ministry of catechesis fosters growth in Catholic faith in all three dimensions—trusting (heart), knowing and believing (mind), and doing (will). The goal should be to have all Catholic youth involved in some program of catechesis" (*Renewing the Vision*).

The bishops go on to remind us that when it comes to planning adolescent catechesis, we must be sure that our efforts

- are developmentally appropriate
- speak to needs, interests, and concerns of adolescents
- are faithful to the core contents of the *Catechism of the Catholic Church*
- enable and empower teens to live their faith in today's world
- connect with the life experience of teens
- employ engaging learning processes and methodologies
- involve group participation
- include parents and provide support for them
- are sensitive and responsive to multicultural realities
- invite young people to explore their own call to ministry

In 2008, the U.S. bishops approved and published a document, created by their Committee on Evangelization and Catechesis, titled *Doctrinal Elements of a Curriculum Framework for the Development of Catechetical Materials for Young People of High School Age*. The purpose of this document was to further assist those responsible for adolescent catechesis in providing formation that is full, complete, and faithful. The Curriculum Framework provides a four-year, eight-semester course of study (six core courses and five electives) for Catholic high schools. In 2010, the bishops followed with an adaptation for parish adolescent catechesis and youth ministry programs. The bishops explain:

The Curriculum Framework is designed to provide systematic content to guide the catechetical formation of young people of high school age in the various catechetical contexts in which it takes place. In particular, this Adaptation is now offered to guide the use of the Curriculum Framework in parish religious education programs, and in catechetical formation that is a constitutive part of youth ministry programs. (Preamble to *Adaptation of the Doctrinal Elements of a Curriculum Framework for the Development of Catechetical Materials for Young People of High School Age*)

The Framework consists of the following core courses of study:

1. The Revelation of Jesus Christ in Scripture
2. Who Is Jesus Christ?
3. The Mission of Jesus Christ—The Paschal Mystery
4. Jesus Christ's Mission Continues in the Church
5. Sacraments as Privileged Encounters with Jesus Christ
6. Life in Jesus Christ

The elective courses of study include the following:

- Sacred Scripture
- History of the Catholic Church
- Living as a Disciple of Jesus Christ in Society
- Responding to the Call of Jesus Christ
- Ecumenical and Interreligious Issues

The Curriculum Framework, according to Norbertine priest Fr. Alfred McBride, "gives coherence, order and structure to [God's great] love story" (*American Magazine*, "A Sturdy Framework: A Defense of the Bishops' New High School Catechesis," September 28, 2009).

The Wild World of Adolescent Catechesis Today

In each era and in various cultures, the transition that today is referred to as "adolescence" is marked by certain behaviors, attitudes, fashions, trends, speech, and idiosyncrasies. Some cultures address this coming-of-age phase through rituals, rites of passage, and small indulgences. What in the past was considered wild behavior, objectionable music, or risqué clothing can seem mild, if not ridiculous, today. Yet, in every era, this reaction to adolescent behaviors simply reflects the adults' desire to guide their young to maturity, unharmed.

Research that generated the *Renewing the Vision* document indicates that the challenges young people face today exacerbate the issues that keep teenagers' parents and adult leaders awake at night. The research reveals the following social trends:

- Many adults no longer feel responsible for youth outside their family.

- Parents are living increasingly hectic lifestyles, and are less available and not as knowledgeable about or intimately involved in their children's daily lives.

- Adults have become uncomfortable communicating moral values or enforcing boundaries for appropriate behavior.

- U.S. society is becoming more age-segregated.

- Families, schools, parishes, and other traditional socializing systems are now more isolated, competitive, and suspicious of one another.

- Mass media has more influence than ever on young people's attitudes, values, and standards.

- Responsibility for young people is increasingly being relinquished to professionals.

These trends contradict Church teaching and common sense. There is a running theme of isolation, which is the antithesis of Christ's command for a loving community that cares for the corporal and spiritual needs of all its members. Another theme is the disruption and undermining of the family's influence. That message is projected in many popular films and television shows in which young people have all the answers, and parents, if present at all, are portrayed as bumbling idiots. This is a major departure from entertainment in which parents would offer credible advice.

Navigating the Sea of Religious Diversity

In view of these influences, it should be no surprise that the religious attitudes of teens are all over the map. This is especially acute in households where faith plays little or no part in family life or where parents are of different faiths or are culturally affiliated with a faith but do not practice it. The higher rates of divorce, blended families, and single parenting are other contributing conditions.

Religiosity studies reveal that approximately 60 percent of American teenagers are either unaffiliated with any religion or are only minimally engaged. Among those who are committed, however, there is movement toward becoming "missionary disciples." This descriptor captures the Church's greatest hope—that evangelization will cultivate new disciples whose mission is to cultivate more disciples, as described in *Evangelii Gaudium: The Joy of the Gospel* (Pope Francis, 2016).

Spiritual but Not Religious (NONEs)

At face value, this trendy expression may appear self-explanatory. Basically, individuals in this category operate out of the belief that each person can be his or her own spiritual authority. Yet some researchers have identified five types of individuals with very different motivations who fit this description:

- *Dissenters*, some of whom are protesting or angry at the Church, while others are just drifting.
- *Casuals*, whose use of certain teachings, spiritual practices, or guides helps them feel better but may not deepen their affinity for God.
- *Explorers*, who are like spiritual tourists enjoying the journey but not intending to settle anywhere; they may mix and match beliefs and practices.
- *Seekers*, who try to find a new form of religious expression or reclaim a former religious experience.
- *Immigrants*, who abandon one faith for another.

In addition to the above MOs, researchers such as Linda Mercadante, author of *Belief without Borders,* have pinpointed six theological positions found in organized religions that are rejected by NONEs, as well as by a lot of today's generation of teenagers, even those who attend church services regularly. These are

1. Exclusivism that rejects all but one's own religion
2. Wrathful or interventionist God
3. Static, permanent afterlife of glorious heaven and torturous hell
4. Oppressively authoritarian religious tradition
5. Nonexperiential, repressive religious community
6. A view of humans as being born bad

Such attitudes can paint the Church and its members as bigoted and out of touch. More important, they can be stumbling blocks to forming a meaningful relationship with Jesus. An example of a more effective approach to teaching seeking or cynical young people was offered by a religious-educator friend of mine who works with teenagers daily. It reflects the praxis of reaching the heart, mind, and will of apprentice disciples.

1. The mentor must be genuine and confident in his or her faith.

2. Give teens interactive opportunities to discuss information and ideas. Use games and simulation activities that make the learning less abstract for minds that are gaining capacity to empathize and grasp more complex concepts.

3. Facilitate teens' ability to think deeply, analyze critically, and explore their questions about faith and the world. Ignore their resistance to this.

4. Encourage the exploration of ideas and questions for which the mentor does not have ready answers. This does not devalue preparation but, rather, emphasizes the need for courage and humility. Welcome the movement of the Holy Spirit.

5. Intentionally incorporate Scripture and Church teaching in your interactions with teens and help them apply Scripture and Church teaching to their experiences.

As catechetical leaders, we need to do our best to understand the secular cultural milieu our young people live in and mentor them with integrity into a deeper, more relevant faith.

Getting Ready for Confirmation

In many U.S. dioceses, the sacrament of confirmation is conferred in adolescence. This is a logical response to the multifaceted changes young people experience at this stage—physical, intellectual, psychological, emotional, and moral. They are now more capable of understanding the commitment to the Christian faith and actively seek answers to many pressing questions about life, specifically theirs. It is an opportunity to accompany youth through a spiritual rite of passage, if they are willing. At the same time, it is imperative to remember that confirmation is not a simple teen-to-adult rite of passage, nor is it a sacrament of maturity. It is a sacrament of initiation.

Confirmation during adolescence is viewed by some as an intervention, a means of directing this natural stage of adolescent development toward the path of spiritual growth. Some parents and catechetical leaders may use confirmation as a carrot to keep teens in the Church. They sense this is their last chance to solidify the early lessons or to help those in need of adjusting their attitudes. This is often where desperation enters.

Warning: Cramming confirmation preparation into a brief time frame in a classroom setting does not create disciples of Christ. Catechetical programs must not imitate high school graduation. Otherwise, adolescents will continue to receive the sacrament and then disappear from the Church.

Service and Justice Ministry

Generally, confirmation programs involve young people in random service projects or the logging of required service hours. This approach can be counterproductive if young people do not see us, the adults of the parish, also embracing service to those in need, charitable works, and works of mercy and social justice as a lifestyle. In such cases, it is understandable that teens will view these required hours as comparable to "community service," which is given as a punishment in lieu of jail time! Often, young people have a sense of fairness and concern for others that we can develop further during this period with skilled and thoughtful preparation.

Likewise, it is becoming more common for public schools to require service. This will prompt teens to ask, "How is the service we do through the Church any different from the service we do for public school?" Ultimately, the service we do at public school is designed to create good citizens—certainly a worthwhile activity. But the service we do as a member of the Church is designed to help teens encounter Christ and to form them into disciples.

It is vitally important that we place service and justice ministry in the context of theological reflection on the gospel and Catholic social teaching. Our responses should address young people's genuine needs and promote their deeper reflection.

Beyond Confirmation—What's Next?

The *National Directory for Catechesis* sums it up in this way: "The most effective catechetical programs for adolescents are integrated into a comprehensive program of pastoral ministry for youth that includes catechesis, community life, evangelization, justice and service, leadership development, pastoral care, and prayer and worship" (*NDC*, #48D).

Adolescents' moods, behaviors, and attitudes are at times (quite often) difficult to understand or accept. Body, mind, and spirit are all in transition. Teens are in the process of trying on identities in search of a good fit. They experience the challenges of seeking intimacy while asserting independence from family and authority figures, of uncovering that which is profound (amazing) while persevering through the mundane. They also battle competing impulses to be good and to be bad. Teens were born to test limits.

So, make your parish's confirmation preparation more effective by combining it with a vital teen-ministry program. Incorporate some fun, food, and fellowship into their continued spiritual formation! Moreover, a loving and welcoming atmosphere is significant. Given the many serious challenges teens face today, this should be a safe place for all, characterized by "warmth, trust, acceptance, and care, so that young people can hear and respond to God's call" (*NDC*, #48D).

Catechetical leaders also can do a great service by helping parents and guardians build the courage to speak from their faith foundation. That is, help them to speak the truth in love and with God-given authority. Intergenerational group settings are conducive to young people witnessing the faith lived out. Sharing personal narratives and group activities can be potent antidotes to the myopia induced by age segregation. I personally enjoyed one such enriching experience of intergenerational catechesis while preparing young people for the sacrament of confirmation. Our team approach relied on the candidates, their sponsors, and a family member—a parent, grandparent, older sibling, or cousin. Everyone had an assignment for each session, including leading prayer, making reminder phone calls, and bringing refreshments. Our youth as well as the adults took responsibility for the teaching. Often, a candidate and his or her sponsor planned the teaching segments together. As a bonus, the adults learned along with the youth.

The hope of confirmation is that following the reception of the sacrament, youth will act on their professed commitment to God and commit to living as disciples of Jesus Christ. This process really begins with baptism, which the Second Vatican Council instructed "should be seen as the root that determines the identity of Christians as disciples of Jesus, that vitalizes their lifelong growth into holiness of life" (Thomas Groome, *Will There Be Faith?*, 77).

Individual Support and Mentoring

Continuing formation of adolescents can and should be customized to meet the needs and interests of youth today. In *Reimagining Faith Formation for the 21st Century: Engaging All Ages and Generations*, John Roberto describes a method of individualizing confirmation preparation that is easily adaptable to continuous post-confirmation catechesis. Roberto suggests utilizing a "confirmation network." Think of a group of young apprentice disciples who learn about the faith together through individual and group activities by tapping into online resources, video clips, and in-person interviews with other young people who have been confirmed. This resource network enables apprentice disciples to learn content from various activities and resources that support their particular, real-time faith journey. In this method, confirmation preparation is not simply initiated when a youngster reaches a specified age or grade in school, but it is done with active discernment, along with a sponsor or another mentor. The apprentice disciple then proceeds with activities and ongoing reflection in a variety of settings and formats—individually, with a mentor, and in community. This approach can integrate a mixture of online and face-to-face encounters that are natural, flexible, and appealing methodologies for youth today.

A Comprehensive Vision

The renewed framework for Catholic youth ministry describes several themes that a comprehensive vision will incorporate. It should be developmentally appropriate, family-friendly, multicultural, intergenerational, and a community-wide collaboration. And it should develop young leaders with programming that is flexible and adaptable. Some of these themes have already been discussed in this chapter; a few warrant more attention below, and I want to add one more new area—technology—to incorporate into your youth ministry.

Intergenerational—Most teens project a persona that they "know things," such as what everyone else is doing, wearing, thinking, etc. In fact, they really know little to nothing about these things but may be afraid to ask. Doing shared ministry and having conversations with adults of varying ages and experiences can open more doors for teens to faith experiences and furnish answers to their unasked questions. It is not unusual for youth to discreetly seek a second opinion from a trusted adult about what their parents have said.

Leadership—By the time young people reach adolescence, many of them are capable of taking on more responsibility for several areas of their life, including their faith development. Although they may creatively dodge invitations to step up and become actively involved, this is an integral step in the discipleship-formation process. People learn best by doing. As with driving lessons, they must sit in the driver's seat with the motor running, put the transmission gear in the drive position, and, at some point, press a foot on the accelerator.

Multicultural—Informing youth that the term *catholic* means "universal" should also bring into focus the diversity of our society and of the Catholic world in particular. It is necessary to expose youth of all ethnic groups to the universality of the faith and the diverse expressions of Catholicism as experienced by people from different cultural backgrounds. Generally, youth today have more exposure to different cultures than did their parents. Inculturation (evangelization of cultures) is one of the tasks of evangelization. Effective moral formation will prepare adolescents to respect others and appreciate diversity as a gift from God.

Technology—*Renewing the Vision* was issued before the emergence of mobile devices and social media, which have had a profound influence on human interaction. Digital, satellite, and emerging technologies are generating new social networks and interactions. "Information is now portable, participatory and personal" (John Roberto, *Reimagining Faith Formation for the 21st Century*). This technology allows people to connect with others who share their preferences, interests, and aspirations. Within these loose networks, the individual is the focus, not the family or community. Yet we and our teens crave community and struggle to find or create it. We must use technology to engage young people, always helping them connect with real people and relationships.

The Joy of Adolescent Catechesis

Of particular importance and help for you as a catechetical leader working with adolescents is the document *The Joy of Adolescent*

Catechesis, a collaborative effort among the National Federation for Catholic Youth Ministry, National Catholic Education Association, and The National Conference for Catechetical Leadership. This resource articulates a shared vision for all who work in faith formation with youth and serves to inform, inspire, and challenge those who lead adolescent catechesis. This valuable resource does not shy away from the challenges of working with youth in the area of faith formation but, rather, offers encouragement and support to those who lead adolescent catechesis so that they might help young people fall more deeply in love with Jesus Christ.

Summary: Forming Wise Disciples

The foolish ones, when taking their lamps, brought no oil with them, but the wise brought flasks of oil with their lamps. (Matt. 25:3–4, NABRE)

In Jesus' parable of the ten virgins awaiting the bridegroom, five of the women were prepared with extra oil, and five foolishly let their lamps run out of oil. All of us, including young people, do foolish things from time to time. Some young people will respond and be ready; others will arrive late, or at least we hope they do. Parents, grandparents, prayer warriors, youth ministers, and catechetical leaders all do their part to insure safe passage from their youth into adulthood.

Catechesis is not a vaccine against teen pregnancy, alcohol abuse, suicide, cyberbullying, or other dangers. The influence of the family, generational transmission of faith beliefs, popular culture, and free will all strongly shape young people's attitudes about God and religion. However, effective catechesis can be a channel for the continued movement of the Holy Spirit in their lives, a movement that began in baptism. Today's approach to adolescent faith formation, more than ever, needs to focus on the three goals: empowering young people to live as disciples of Jesus Christ in our world today; drawing young people to responsible participation in the life, mission, and work of the

Catholic faith community; and fostering the total personal and spiritual growth of each young person.

For Reflection and Discussion

- What hope do you see in the faces of adolescents in your catechetical setting—in those you have observed since infancy and in others who are newcomers?
- How would you describe their current challenges, as you understand them?
- Is your present catechetical program a solid vehicle for this leg of your teenagers' journey to eternity? Does it foster holistic faith development that grows trust, knowledge/belief, and behavior, i.e., heart, mind, and will?

Growing as a Catechetical Leader

The "Young Church" is a wonderfully hopeful moniker, even though there are special challenges in doing ministry with adolescents. Assess your parish's weak links in this ministry area. Are your youth ministry and catechetical ministry wedded in function and goal (whether they are in one structure or not)? Create opportunities for catechists and youth-ministry moderators to cross-fertilize skills. How can you

bridge gaps (if needed) to establish/reinforce a comprehensive youth ministry? Initiate conversation with ministry leaders having any connection with young people to engage the entire faith community.

Collaborate with parish leaders to open the way for young apprentices to act in the ways that Christians behave.

Go to www.loyolapress.com/ECL to access the worksheet.

Suggested Action

Have the group tell a story of what they believe through the creation of a series of memes. Using the Creed or Profession of Faith, line-by-line, have the group create memes, working individually or in pairs or small groups. Share the final product at a parish-wide event or with younger students, e.g., youth in the parish school or religious-education program.

For Further Consideration

The Joy of Adolescent Catechesis. National Federation for Catholic Youth Ministry (Arlington, VA: National Catholic Education Association, 2016).

Reimagining Faith Formation for the 21st Century: Engaging All Ages and Generations. John Roberto (Naugatuck, CT: Lifelong Faith Associates, 2015).

Renewing the Vision: A Framework for Catholic Youth Ministry (Washington, DC: United States Conference of Catholic Bishops, 1997).

Will There Be Faith?: A New Vision for Educating and Growing Disciples. Thomas H. Groome (New York: HarperOne, 2011).

Whole Community Catechesis in Plain English. Bill Huebsch (New London, CT: Twenty-Third Publications, 2002).

8

Let the Children Come to Me: Catechesis for School-Age Children

Magical Expectations

I distinctly recall, as a child, looking up and following the trail of painted cherubs on the ceiling murals above the altar in my church. The cherubic faces were always white, which confused me even then. Nevertheless, I envisioned myself, and others like me, hidden in the clouds of those heavenly scenes. I remember the smooth movement of ushers taking up the collection and, always, the music. Today, I enjoy the old Catholic hymns because I heard them frequently at Mass, along with guitar music that signaled a new era. What are your early memories? Is it the smell of incense, the booming organ, the ringing bells?

From a child's vantage point, the faith experience usually begins with a magical expectation. There are gestures and experiences unique to church: ritual prayers and special vestments, altar cloths and shiny vessels, incense and bells, processions and hymns. These sights and sounds create a sense of wonder and awe for which children have a seemingly unlimited capacity. Their world is filled with heroes and tales of adventure; thus, Bible stories, the lives of saints, and the ministry of Jesus feed young people's religious imagination. Childhood is a natural time for faith formation. And yet our present catechetical system that is centered on the religious instruction of children only is not working today.

We Have a Problem

Modern families are busy! Kids are involved in sports teams, music lessons, dance troupes, and academic enrichment activities—all of which compete heavily with religious-formation programs and often win out. Parents invest precious time and financial resources on carefully selected extra activities that promise advantages for their children, such as academic success, physical health, popularity, and character building. Many sponsoring organizations impose mandatory practices or rehearsals and other stringent requirements. Such multiple commitments, added to school for children and work for the parents (who chauffeur them around), make scheduling a tremendous challenge. Because families are pulled in so many directions, what can result is the perception that faith formation is just one more activity among many.

Dramatic changes in family structure pose another set of challenges. The prevalence of divorce results in many school-age children being shuttled back and forth between their parents' homes from week to week. To compound this, children of divorce must adapt to the nuances of family life in multiple households, with different rules, expectations, and relationship dynamics. Other family configurations—such as single parents, same-sex and cohabiting partners, and married parents with fragile or dysfunctional relationships—all present alternatives that challenge official Church teaching.

So, how does today's family life affect catechesis? How does it reinforce or erode a child's view of God as a faithful, loving, and dependable Father? These are questions we as catechetical leaders must reflect on.

Children Do Not Learn Faith in a Vacuum

Traditionally, enrollment in religious-education programs has been highest for school-age children. Catechists are more readily committed to the service of faith-sharing with primary and elementary school-age youth than with any other age group. Often, parents and grandparents take on the teaching task. There is an abundance of faith-formation materials for school-age youth. Furthermore, the faith questions that young children ask (and need answered) may be "easier" to address than questions proposed by adults. The goal of family and catechetical leaders appears to be, "Lay a good foundation and they will not stray—far."

Despite substantial investment in youth catechesis, current religiosity studies conclude that the Church is losing more young disciples between childhood and adolescence than among adolescents and young adults (John Roberto, *Reimagining Faith Formation for the 21st Century*). In other words, by the time children leave elementary school, many have left the Church mentally, even if they are not gone physically.

Perhaps the first thing we can do to address the challenges we face in catechesis for school-age children is to admit that there can no longer be such a thing as "child catechesis." There can only be catechesis of *children and their families*. We must embrace the fact that in doing children's faith formation today, we must address the needs of the entire family. Children do not learn faith in a vacuum. For too long, we have been attempting to instill beliefs, values, and practices in children without the support that families and communities once provided. Any talk of children's faith formation must be a conversation about family faith formation.

Effective Catechesis for Children and Families

The solution, of course, is not to abandon children's faith formation. On the contrary, studies continue to show that the seeds of a solid and long-lasting faith are sown in the early stages of life. As much as we are called to give priority to adult faith formation, the overriding goal is to create families and communities where those adults are more fully equipped to instill faith in others and especially in their children.

With that in mind, let's identify some key principles you will need to rely on as a catechetical leader when it comes to catechizing children and families.

1. **Provide structure and sound doctrine.** Children need structure in their lives. A key to success in any child/family catechesis format is to provide a structure that helps the family establish a routine. Better yet, help parents turn the routine into a ritual, so that young people recognize the priority and centrality of their faith formation. Likewise, it is crucial to use resources that are not only engaging for children and families but are also faithful to Church teaching. The U.S. Catholic bishops have a stringent process for approving written resources for catechesis, and you would do well to ensure that families are using resources that are in conformity with the *Catechism of the Catholic Church*. While a variety of resources are available, including online and video, it is always important to have a written text to refer to in order to have the most complete and accurate verbiage about the Catholic faith.

2. **Avoid academic model/approach.** It bears repeating that faith formation is not the teaching of a subject or topic; rather, it is an encounter with the Living Word of God, Jesus Christ. Any child/family faith-formation programs should avoid a strictly academic approach to transmitting the faith. While faith formation does have a crucial intellectual component to it, such knowledge must

take root within the context of an affective relationship with Jesus Christ—something that is fostered and supported primarily through experiences of prayer.

3. **Think intergenerationally.** Children need to learn from their peers, their near-peers, and adults. In order to apprentice young people into the Catholic way of life, it is necessary to have adults present to serve as mentors. Likewise, elders such as grandparents serve as important role models and transmitters of wisdom and Catholic practices for young people as they strive to integrate the teachings of Jesus and the traditions of the Church into their lives.

4. **Have high expectations of parents and empower them.** For too long, we have communicated to parents that they can drop their kids off at the parish and pick them up "when they're Catholic." The structures in society that once supported a "drop-off" model for faith formation are no longer in place. As a result, every effort must be made to involve parents in the experience of forming their children in faith. Parents remain the most significant influence in the formation of their children. As a catechetical leader, your job is to communicate expectations to parents, assure them of support, and empower them to be able to embrace their role as their child's primary educator.

5. **Include service and mission.** There is no need to wait until youngsters begin sacrament preparation to invite their participation in most aspects of the Church's mission. Even very young children can appreciate helping others in need. School-age children are capable of understanding that Jesus' love for people was expressed in his words, actions, and attitude toward others. They can model love in action as evident in the lives of the Blessed Mother, Saint Joseph, the disciples, and the saints. Furthermore, children may witness compassionate outreach done

by a family member who checks in on elderly or homebound neighbors.

Catechesis for service and justice goes beyond doing "good works." It helps young disciples cultivate conscience through a Christian identity that embraces compassion, mercy, reconciliation, and peace. With reflection and practice, youth will cultivate genuine concern for the well-being of others, which can be applied at home, in school, and in the world. Service and justice should be anchored in prayer, rooted in Scripture, and grounded in the sacraments—particularly baptism, Eucharist, and reconciliation. Always incorporate prayer and reflection time for children during their service assignments. Introduce young children to The Two Feet of Love in Action—Charity and Justice (USCCB). Teach older children how to use the Pastoral Circle (See-Judge-Act) reflection process to understand social problems in light of the gospel.

6. **Imbue faith-formation experiences with prayer.** The *General Directory for Catechesis* tells us that catechesis is most effective in achieving its ends when it takes place within a climate of prayer. This means much more than beginning and ending faith-formation experiences with the perfunctory recitation of a traditional prayer. Rather, it means that young people must be invited to truly encounter Jesus in prayer that is reflective and enables them to dwell in silence and speak/listen to Jesus in the silence of their hearts.

7. **Create a sense of mystery, wonder, and awe.** Children are naturals when it comes to the world of mystery, since they still have a sense of wonder and awe that has not been inhibited by the reason and logic of adulthood. As a result, faith formation should incorporate a sense of mystery that can be experienced only through prayer and the language of mystery, which includes

silence, ritual, signs, symbols, music, and storytelling, to name a few.

With regards to storytelling, an overriding goal should be for children to come to know the story of salvation history and to own it as their own story. Likewise, children are fascinated with heroes and stories of adventure, of which there is no dearth in Scripture and in the lives of the saints. Include the witness of young people like themselves, as well as saints from all regions of the world. It is imperative that the witness of women of faith be presented. For example, teach them about Queen Esther, Veronica on the road to Calvary, and qualities of the virtuous woman described in Proverbs 31. Supplement lessons with sacred and inspirational art, music, poetry, and film. Incorporate nature. Encourage children's personal expressions.

8. **Connect to the Eucharist.** At the center of the Catholic way of life is the Eucharist. Faith formation must flow from and lead to the celebration of the Eucharist on Sunday. All of us who are baptized are baptized for one reason: to enable us to come to the Lord's Table and to be fed and nourished by word and sacrament. We are incapable of sustaining ourselves, and it is through Jesus Christ—whom we encounter most profoundly in the Eucharist—that "we live and move and have our being." All faith-formation efforts should foster a greater desire and appreciation for the Eucharist.

9. **Offer options and flexibility.** Families today are facing challenges the likes of which have never been seen before, and family life is more hectic and complex than ever. As a result, a "one size fits all" approach to faith formation will not work. While you cannot meet the specific and unique needs of every family in your program, it is imperative that you offer options and have a sense of flexibility that respects the busyness and complexities of family life.

10. **Pay attention to diverse learning styles.** In his book *Frames of Mind: The Theory of Multiple Intelligences* (New York: Basic Books, 2011), Howard Gardner explains that people learn in a variety of ways, and so we need to provide varied learning experiences. This is especially true when working with children in faith formation. Be sure to incorporate varied activities that emphasize the following learning styles:

   a. *Words*—for children who learn best through reading, writing, and discussion
   b. *Music*—for children who have a good sense of rhythm and melody and love to sing, hum, chant, or rap
   c. *Logic/Math*—for children who tend to think in numbers and patterns and love to solve problems
   d. *Vision and Space*—for children who tend to think in images and pictures and enjoy making posters, collages, graphs, charts, or other displays
   e. *Body*—for children who are well coordinated and enjoy using gestures, body language, and hands-on activities
   f. *Nature*—for children who are keenly aware of the natural world and learn best when content is related to nature
   g. *People*—for children who learn best by interacting with others and enjoy cooperative learning experiences (groups and pairings)
   h. *Self*—for children who are introspective, enjoy quiet time alone, and learn best when given time to process information on their own

Parable of the Ten Talents

I have strong early memories of church that include dressing up in my Sunday best, the family piling into the car, avoiding cracks in the vinyl kneelers, favoring certain priests, and anticipating waffles after Mass. However, a particular faith experience lingers in my memory. I remember well a gregarious young priest who stepped down to the level of the congregation. He announced that the parish would establish a Children's Mass. I don't recall Fr. G's actual message but his interpretation of the parable of the talents, a story in which someone distributed coins (talents) unevenly. One person received ten, one person received five, and another received only one coin. This impressed upon me the serious nature of using what God gave me. I wondered how many talents God had given to me, and I promised not to bury them. My religious imagination had been ignited.

"The most important task of the catechesis of children is to provide, through the witness of adults, an environment in which young people can grow in faith" (*NDC*, #48E). Ideally, faith grows as a natural beat in the rhythm of family life. Like other family practices and routines—such as brushing teeth at bedtime, washing hands before eating, family vacations in summer, first day of school photos—family prayer and other traditions become the norm. We just know this is the way things are done, until we leave home base and learn of different possibilities.

Conscience Formation

Do you remember what sin looked and felt like as a child? Perhaps early moral challenges involved hiding the truth, eating meat on a day of abstinence, delighting in gossip, or excluding a classmate during recess. Fear of punishment or disapproval from authority figures, such as parents, grandparents, and teachers, usually deters very young children. Responding to that motivation, the developing conscience of a young child can cause her or him to avoid and/or regret "bad" behavior.

Usually by age seven, which the Church has deemed the "age of reason," children are capable of distinguishing right from wrong, and their consciences are just beginning to emerge. The parents' faith, attitude toward other human beings, and trust in a loving God strongly influence the development of the child's faith (*NDC*). This formation of conscience, which begins at home, is extended through religious-formation programs. It is strengthened by shared faith experiences in liturgy, prayer, and service to others. Introducing catechesis outside the home is intended to be a bridge between the domestic church and the parish faith community rather than a substitute for either.

What happens when behavior in the home contradicts lessons received in religious education or the message from the pulpit—and vice versa? I've witnessed far too many situations where children attend religious education while their parents are at Mass (an inexcusable scheduling conflict on the part of the parish). Or children are dropped off for religious education, retrieved afterwards, and no one attends Mass. Or children arrive late and unprepared for faith formation. This parental behavior models half-hearted efforts at faith and implies that religious matters take lower priority. The challenge for today's catechetical leader is to create a structure and format for faith formation that communicates its centrality, priority, and significance for the well-being of the entire family.

Children find rituals and routines both intriguing and comforting, even if they experience boredom in the process. Effective catechesis can reveal the mysteries of faith that religious rituals signify. Understanding can be fast-tracked and deepened when youth are engaged in communal practices of liturgical celebrations, prayer services, and learning activities that serve as portals to understanding sacred truths.

The Young Church of Today

The idea that we see children only as "the Church of the future" is passé. They are part of the Church *now*! As the *National Directory for Catechesis* guides, "Children have a dignity of their own. . . . [T]hey are important not only for what they will do in the future, but for who they are now" (*NDC*, #48E). Along with muscles and bones, a child's moral conscience is growing. Young people have an influence on their friends, siblings, and parents in the present. Some are beginning to discern a vocation as they dream about the future. Many are discovering and testing their ability in science, math, sports, the arts, and other areas. For all of us, human development in all dimensions is a lifelong journey, and how we live out our faith always touches others.

Summary: What Do You See?

While they were looking intently at the sky as he was going, suddenly two men dressed in white garments stood beside them. They said, "Men of Galilee, why are you standing there looking at the sky?"
(Acts 1:10–11a, NABRE)

The *National Directory for Catechesis* synthesizes the guidance and challenge of catechizing older children in this way: "Assist them in the praxis of observing, exploring, interpreting and evaluating their experiences; in learning to ascribe a Christian meaning to their lives; and in learning to act according to the norms of faith and love—the presence in today's society of many conflicting values makes it all the more important to help young people to interiorize authentic values" (*NDC*, #48E).

Despite the mountainous resources invested in children's catechesis, the Church is losing more young people between childhood and adolescence than between adolescence and young adulthood—even though the younger group is more or less a captive audience, since they do not drive and are dependent on parental decisions about how they spend their time. The chasm between abstract concepts of faith and mysterious religious practices on the one hand, and the praxis of an active, living faith on the other, can be filled by a new vision and methodology.

Today's youths are immersed in technology. This fact, along with their erratic schedules at home, support the integration of new teaching aids such as online study assignments, prayer, and Bible apps for their mobile devices. A maturing faith is propelled by a growing desire for deeper knowledge of the truth of faith (*NDC*). Thus, the catechetical curriculum should be **contextual**—"addressing the needs, hungers, interests and concerns of people today and their unique spiritual and faith journeys by embracing an approach that moves from *life* to *faith* to *life*" (Roberto, *Reimagining Faith Formation for the 21st Century*). It also should be **multiplatform**—"delivered and conducted in multiple settings—self-directed, mentored, at home, in small groups, in large groups, church-wide, in the community and world—and in physical and online learning environments." It is time to stop gazing at the sky. Instead, look into the eyes and hearts of young people and their caregivers. Help them to recognize that the gospel is still the best news for their world and ours today.

For Reflection and Discussion

- What are the strongest memories of your own childhood faith formation?
- Why is it appropriate to say that we should no longer speak of "child catechesis" but only of catechesis of children and their families?
- Is your parish program capable of going beyond the school model? How can you and your team creatively incorporate new principles and teach to children's learning styles?

- How can you as a catechetical leader equip and empower parents to embrace their role as their children's primary educator? What kind of help do parents most need?

Growing as a Catechetical Leader

Consider some of the thorniest issues your children's catechetical program faces. Are there specific ways that involving parents could enhance the program? How could the youth catechetical program spiritually feed parents (caregivers)? Are there opportunities for parallel study? Is there a comfortable and inviting place for adults to gather for discussion or presentations on topics similar to those the youth are studying but at a deeper level? What are the interests of each group of parents? Who else on the pastoral team should be consulted to coordinate catechetical opportunities for parents? Engaging parents is a vital approach to assisting them to effectively catechize their children.

Go to www.loyolapress.com/ECL to access the worksheet.

Suggested Action

God does not hand out report cards, detention slips, or gold stars. Rather, he invites children to come to him, to talk together, to trust and follow his lead. Taking the long view of catechesis as a lifelong journey, make a list of things you are doing today that emphasizes this invitation from God over content mastery. Identify further steps you can take to create an atmosphere in which children can hear God calling them by name. Now, state one action you will take this season to modify your approach to more effectively catechize school-age children.

For Further Consideration

Reimagining Faith Formation for the 21st Century: Engaging All Ages and Generations. John Roberto (Naugatuck, CT: Lifelong Faith Associates, 2015).

United States Conference of Catholic Bishops, Secretariat of Evangelization and Catechesis at http://www.usccb.org.

Will There Be Faith? A New Vision for Educating and Growing Disciples. Thomas H. Groome (New York: HarperOne, 2011).

9

Bridging the Gap: Catechesis for Persons with Special Needs

As he passed by he saw a man blind from birth. His disciples asked him, "Rabbi, who sinned, this man or his parents, that he was born blind?" Jesus answered, "Neither he nor his parents sinned; it is so that the works of God might be made visible through him."
(John 9:1–3, NABRE)

I Once Was Clueless

My first assignment as a young catechist was a combined class of third and fourth graders. A mother approached me during class to ask if I would accept her child with my group. I said yes, and a look of relief washed over her face. The handsome boy with a twisted body sat calmly in his wheelchair. Michael was older than the other students. He had multiple disabilities and was nonverbal. I am confident that acceptance was the right answer. Nonetheless, I was clueless about how to include youth with special needs such as these in class activities. More important, I had no idea how to share the faith with Michael. Did he understand the concepts? How did he process the lessons? From what I knew, this was his introduction to religious education outside the home.

Through the years, I received nominal training for catechizing persons with different physical, intellectual, or sensory needs. I learned some basic American Sign Language. On archdiocesan catechetical days, I chose to attend a special-needs workshop or two. However, the lack of guidance continued to bother me when I became a catechetical leader. Fortunately, today there is support for catechetical leaders in this realm.

ADA Comes to Church

Broad advocacy for persons with a range of disabilities is a relatively recent social approach. Passage of the Americans with Disabilities Act (ADA) in 1990 helped raise awareness and sensitivity across sectors of society—in the workplace, public spaces, and academic institutions. The tide of advocacy also generated local church responses. Examples of parochial action include an annual White Mass for people with special needs, providing sign language interpreters at parish and diocesan events, and modifying facilities to add ramps, elevators, and handicapped-accessible restrooms.

In 2016, the National Catholic Partnership on Disability (NCPD) commissioned a special report on "Disabilities in Parishes Across the United States: How Parishes in the United States Accommodate and Serve People with Disabilities" (Center for Applied Research in the Apostolate [CARA]). This report disclosed five encouraging key findings:

- 96 percent of parishes have a wheelchair-accessible entrance.
- 43 percent of churches have a list of resources to refer people with disabilities to for professional help.
- 72 percent of parishes have people with disabilities who volunteer for the parish.
- 93 percent of parishes offer accommodations to allow those with disabilities to participate in parish social events.
- 63 percent of parishes adapt their current resources for students with disabilities.

According to the U.S. Census Bureau, nearly one in five Americans has a disability. That's more than 55 million people. NCPD also reports that one in three families has someone with a disability. Disability crosses economic, racial, regional, and religious lines. These figures may seem surprising. Yet the scope of the referenced CARA report paints a clearer picture. CARA's study included persons with sensory, physical, and intellectual impairments, autism, mental illnesses, chronic illnesses, age-related disabilities, and veterans with a war-related injury. All these individuals have special needs. How does the parish, academic, or other institution where you minister evaluate them?

Even as our awareness of and language for this matter evolve, Church teaching is unambiguous concerning the duty to catechize persons with special needs: "As far as their condition allows, catechetical formation is given to the mentally and physically handicapped" (*Code of Canon Law*, #777.4). The *National Directory for Catechesis* adds, "All persons with disabilities have the capacity to proclaim the Gospel and to be living witnesses to its truth within the community of faith and offer valuable gifts. Their involvement enriches every aspect of Church life. They are not just the recipients of catechesis—they are also its agents. . . . Every person, however limited, is capable of growth in holiness" (*NDC*, #49).

Pope Francis emphasized the stigma of disabilities during a liturgy in Rome, saying, "We are familiar with the objections raised . . . to a life characterized by serious physical limitations. It is thought that sick or disabled persons cannot be happy, since they cannot live the lifestyle held up by the culture of pleasure and entertainment" (Jubilee for the Sick and Persons with Disabilities, June 12, 2016). But to the priest (and, by extension, the parishioner) who does not welcome everyone, the pope says, "Close the doors of the church! Either everyone or no one."

It's Personal

A close friend of mine who has loved Scripture from his youth was born with a disability affecting his limbs. He says people often make false assumptions about his capabilities. One time an airline flight attendant insisted on stowing his crutches overhead, when he could have done it himself. He laments never being invited to serve as lector at Mass, as were other members of the parish teen group. There are countless heartbreaking stories of parents whose child with special needs was refused sacrament preparation and the family subsequently left the Church.

The 2016 CARA report also revealed that over 90 percent of pastors are aware of someone with a disability in their parish. However, two factors influence their response: (1) parish size/location and (2) participation of parishioners with disabilities in ministerial roles or parish committees. The responses disclosed that although a majority of parishes have accessible entrances and parking, only 51 percent reported having a wheelchair-accessible sanctuary, which limits ministry participation at Mass.

Holy Scripture presents Jesus' attitude toward persons with disabilities in the following passages:

- man born blind (John 9)
- child possessed by a demon (Mark 7)
- woman with a hemorrhage (Matt. 9)
- mute person (Matt. 9)
- man with a withered hand (Mark 3)
- leper (Luke 5)

There are many more episodes. Jesus not only healed people's physical or mental states but also spoke to them with dignity, forgave their sins, and taught them about our heavenly Father. Jesus said we must become like little children—not childish, but childlike (see Mark

10:13–16). "Physical access for persons with disability is important, but attitudes of openness, value, and welcome are crucial" (Janice Benton, OFS, and Nancy Thompson, OCDS, "Making Room for Persons with Disabilities" [USCCB, 2015]).

From Concern to Compassion to Justice

Contrary to popular and prolific images, each and every one of us is in some way disabled, malformed, stunted, ill, and dying. But some limitations are more obvious or debilitating than others. As a result of cultural conditioning, individuals may feel awkward, ill-equipped, or fearful of engaging persons with special needs. In some cultures, a disability is regarded as a mark of shame in the family, a belief that makes it difficult to bring the loved one to church or other public places. But the Church sees it differently.

> The Church sees in men and women, in every person, the living image of God himself. This image finds, and must always find anew, an ever deeper and fuller unfolding of itself in the mystery of Christ, the Perfect Image of God, the One who reveals God to man and man to himself. . . . Christ, the Son of God, "by his incarnation has united himself in some fashion with every person." (*Compendium of the Social Doctrine of the Church*, #105, Pontifical Council for Justice and Peace, 2004)

Always, the Church uplifts the dignity of the human person. She seeks to proliferate this gospel-based message in countless ways. The Church has articulated its stance on inclusion of persons with disabilities in numerous documents over the past several decades, as shown in the following chart.

Date	Document	Key Statement(s)
1978	*Pastoral Statement on Persons with Disabilities,* USCC	People with disabilities "seek to serve the community and to enjoy their full baptismal rights as members of the Church" (no. 33); and "The Church finds its true identity when it fully integrates itself with [persons with disabilities]" (no. 12).
1995	*Guidelines for the Celebration of the Sacraments with Persons with Disabilities,* USCCB	"By reason of their Baptism, all Catholics are equal in dignity in the sight of God, and have the same divine calling" (no. 1). Therefore, "Catholics with disabilities have a right to participate in the sacraments as full functioning members of the local ecclesial community" (no. 2).
1997	*General Directory for Catechesis,* USCCB	"Every Christian community considers those who suffer handicaps, physical or mental, as well as other forms of disability—especially children—as persons particularly beloved of the Lord. . . . Education in the faith, which involves the family above all else, calls for personalized and adequate programs" (*GDC*, #189).
1998	*Welcome and Justice for Persons with Disabilities: A Framework of Access and Inclusion,* USCCB	"Catechetical programs should be accessible to persons with disabilities and open to their full, active and conscious participation, according to their capacity" (no. 5). Fellow Christians should "recognize and appreciate the contribution persons with disabilities can make to the Church's spiritual life, and encourage them to do the Lord's work in the world according to their God-given talents and capacity" (no. 7).
2005	*National Directory for Catechesis,* USCCB	The involvement of persons with disabilities "enriches every aspect of Church life. They are not just the recipients of catechesis—they are also its agents" (*NDC*, #49).

| 2011 | *Life Matters: Persons with Disabilities,* USCCB Respect Life Program pamphlet | "In short, as persons with disabilities share their gifts and needs, they bring out the best in our mutual humanity. They challenge us to live the Gospel precepts of charity in the real world, to sacrifice some of our comfort for others, to take the time to enable them to be full members of society. They need to feel our solidarity with them, and to know their true dignity and worth as fellow sisters and brothers in Christ. Our own future with Christ depends on it." |

In 1998, the Catholic bishops of the United States issued the document *Welcome and Justice for Persons with Disabilities.* From that episcopal statement and other Church documents, a ten-point moral framework for reflection and action was created. This can be downloaded for free as the printable resource provided at the end of this chapter.

Upholding the Dignity of Persons with Special Needs

Through the millennia, societies employed numerous means to achieve the same end concerning persons who look different or learn differently. Until recent times, the goal was to remove these persons from the community. Generally, those who were born with birth defects, became disabled, or were chronically ill were abandoned—placed out of sight, kept out of mind. Some were hidden and confined at home, others in the wild. In arctic regions, some frail, elderly people would be placed on ice floes to drift away. Leper colonies have served this purpose from biblical times into the modern era.

Though the strategies may vary today, the intent too often lingers. Advances in medicine, science, and public opinion have improved quality of life and made integration attainable for persons with special needs and their families. There are promising examples of inclusion in media and entertainment. Educational policies to mainstream students with special needs provide opportunities for encounter, empathy, and friendship.

On the other hand, the promotions of euthanasia, assisted suicide, and prenatal testing have insinuated themselves into our modern consciousness. While these are not new ideas, they are gaining a foothold with some sectors of society, due in part to creative marketing and non-gospel values. As a result, persons categorized as disabled continue to face massive discrimination.

The abortion rate for fetuses suspected of having a disability or life-threatening condition ranges from 80 to 94 percent (Benton and Thompson, *Making Room for Persons with Disabilities*, [NCPD, 2015]). Babies born with a disability or life-threatening condition face an increased threat of being allowed to die. And despite automation and supportive technology, persons with disabilities experience a 70 percent unemployment rate.

As Christ's hands and feet, we in the Church can and should provide accommodations for those with the following challenges:

Physical and Sensory—For the visually impaired, we can provide Braille and large-print lectionaries, missals, and other liturgical resources, as well as audio recordings and expanded aural descriptions. Deaf or hearing-impaired individuals may benefit from captioned DVDs/videos, sign language interpretation, and proximate seating. Ramps and height accommodations at the ambo can assist some with physical challenges. Publishers are releasing textbooks and manipulatives for youth with autism and intellectual disabilities. Some catechetical leaders find that symbolic catechesis is useful, when it is necessary to reinforce or replace heavy reliance on language.

Intellectual and Mental-Health—Currently, publishers of catechetical resources provide adaptive materials for persons with Down syndrome and those on the autism spectrum. On a smaller scale, mental-health professionals and advocates are addressing the spiritual needs of persons with mental illness. The latter needs much more attention.

Adaptive Catechesis

Many parents of children with special needs want their child to receive religious education but have encountered a number of obstacles in church and elsewhere. Some parents have heard that their parish lacks the interest, numbers, or resources to establish an adaptive program. Others have grown weary of patronizing attitudes or of being told that their expectations are unrealistic or inconvenient. Still others question whether their child with a developmental disability will ever be able to "grasp" the tenets of the Catholic faith. Some families have given up and fallen away from the Church.

For all these reasons, adaptive catechesis provides an opportunity not only to educate the child but also to promote spiritual healing within families and within the broader community, whose attitudes may have caused pain in the past. Adaptive catechesis not only attends to the child with special needs but also to the experiences and needs of his or her family. Parents often spend a lot of time and energy seeking the best forms of education, community life, and health care for their children. Being welcomed and accepted by a parish community can feel like a well-deserved respite. In addition, adaptive catechesis enables a child to

- become part of a community.
- be known by others as part of the community.
- learn new social skills and develop existing skills.
- build friendships with typically developing peers and others.
- participate in Mass.
- share his or her gifts.

In these ways and others, children learn to experience God's love through relationships. They understand that they are precious, worthy, and beautiful in the eyes of God and in the eyes of the people around them. Catechizing children with special needs is a collaborative effort. At the heart of this collaboration is the child, whose needs and gifts will determine the involvement and interaction of others. Typical roles and responsibilities also include the pastor, you as the catechetical leader, a coordinator for the adaptive program, parents, catechists, aides, and the entire parish community. In your role as the catechetical leader, here are a few things to keep in mind:

- Express the desire to learn from parents and other professionals about a child's gifts and needs.
- Interact directly with the child in ways appropriate to his or her communication style.
- Maintain a warm and open presence to families at liturgies and key program events.
- Create opportunities for parents, siblings, and children to participate in liturgies and other parish events.
- Emphasize that a child with a disability is not spiritually disabled.
- Lead conversations about how the children themselves can serve and participate in the parish, the larger Church, and the world.

Parents Can Be Partners in Adaptive Learning

Having an open, ongoing, and meaningful relationship with parents is crucial when working with a child with special needs. The child's parents know him or her best and have vital information about how to care for and teach their child. Often, there is a team of professionally trained experts working alongside the family "behind the scenes." So remember: *it is not the catechist's role to diagnose or give recommendations regarding the treatment of the child's disability.*

It is important that the catechist learn all he or she can from all the resources the family can provide, tap into all the support available, and help the child learn about and experience faith as fully as possible. When parents first enroll a child with special needs, the program coordinator should immediately enter into the first of many conversations with them and gather as much information as possible about the child. Parents might complete an enrollment form that provides important background about the child, including goals for their child, his or her abilities, learning style, former and current exposure to the faith, and relevant information about the child's disability. The catechist can read this form, then make initial contact with the parents to begin building a relationship with the family and gain additional information and insight into the child's needs.

Multifaceted Assessment

Each child learns, takes in information, and experiences faith differently. Your catechetical programs can use key questions to identify children's needs and strengths.

- How does the child learn best: independently, in a group, or with a partner—such as a same-age peer, a teen faith mentor, or a parent?
- What is the child able to do physically?
- What are the child's communication abilities?
- What concepts or practices come easily to the child? How can the catechist build on those concepts or practices to introduce others?
- Does the child exhibit special physical talents, musical talents, or other creative talents?

- Does the child love to share knowledge about a specific topic?

As the U.S. bishops have stated, the involvement of persons with disabilities "enriches every aspect of Church life. They are not just the recipients of catechesis—they are also its agents" (*NDC*, #49). We are called not only to share the faith with all our sisters and brothers but also to receive their gifts. Adaptive catechesis brings all parties to this table of abundance.

Flexibility Is the Key

Persons with special needs learn best in certain settings and at certain paces and levels. It is important to be flexible and to consult with parents in determining which approach is most suitable for each child. Consider the following:

- **One-on-One Setting**—This format is ideal for those whose disability puts steep limits on their ability to convey understanding or for those who learn best in a controlled environment that is free from distractions that might hinder or undermine the experience. Although such learning takes place in a one-on-one setting, the goal is to provide the learner with the skills he or she needs to enter parish life fully. A one-on-one setting includes the learner and a catechist and may also include an aide (a near-peer) to act as a faith mentor. The instruction is one-on-one, is relationship based, and uses a variety of creative techniques and materials suited to the learner's abilities and needs.

- **Adapted Group Catechesis**—The goal of catechesis for those with disabilities is to provide it in the least restrictive environment possible. This means that inclusivity is paramount. A peer-group setting is ideal for learners who are social, who thrive when working with their peers, and who require simple adaptations of a book-based lesson in order to be able to learn and express their faith while interacting with others. In this group setting, aides, mentors, or other suitable assistants are provided as needed. Basic adaptations and strategies can be used to communicate concepts of the faith in ways suitable and appropriate for the needs of the learner.

The bottom line is, you don't need to be a professional in special education in order to effectively serve those with special needs. However, you and the program coordinator and catechists do need a basic understanding of common developmental conditions and how they affect a person's learning and communication. Then you can create an approach that makes the content of a lesson accessible to those with special needs.

Look for Available Help

Catechists and catechetical leaders should not hesitate to reach out for assistance when addressing the issues of special-needs students. Ask parents for information. Get suggestions from a child's occupational or physical therapist or school personnel. Ask the parents for permission to contact this network to get ideas for working with the child.

Work with parish leadership and your pastor to foster a welcoming parish environment before, during, and after Mass. A welcoming parish community will make faith-formation sessions more satisfying and meaningful. It will likewise create a more accessible environment and offer needed accommodations. Discuss the possibility of celebrating Masses that are adapted for people with disabilities. Research ways in which parishioners with disabilities can serve the parish. The following advocacy groups have a vested interest in assisting individuals with special needs, their families, and those who serve them in faith formation:

- National Catholic Partnership on Disability (NCPD)
- Institute for Pastoral Initiatives, University of Dayton

- National Catholic Office for the Deaf
- Xavier Society for the Blind

Adapting Sacramental-Preparation Programs

Catechetical leaders need to use discretion in all situations but especially with persons who have special needs and may not be capable of verbally articulating their consent or understanding of the sacraments. The Church teaches that when there is doubt, pastors and catechetical leaders should err on the side of allowing the individual to receive the sacrament.

In their 1978 *Guidelines on Celebrating the Sacraments,* the Catholic bishops clarified conditions for receiving the seven sacraments and appropriate accommodations for special needs. The General Principles open with this assertion: "By reason of their Baptism, all Catholics are equal in dignity in the sight of God, and have the same divine calling. Catholics with disabilities have a right to participate in the sacraments as full functioning members of the local ecclesial community" (canon 213). Additionally, "Disability, of itself, is never a reason for deferring Baptism."

Furthermore, the General Principles establish that "the creation of a fully accessible parish reaches beyond mere physical accommodation to encompass the attitudes of all parishioners towards persons with disabilities." This is best done in consultation with persons who have special needs, their caregivers, family, and advocates. At times, it is more feasible for parishes to collaborate in supporting parishioners with special needs.

We have a duty to catechize all people with disabilities who reside within the parish boundaries. Some of these folks live in isolated conditions. Make plans to visit and welcome those who live in nursing facilities and group homes. You can adjust your catechetical program to meet such needs through making pastoral visits, arranging transportation to the parish, and hosting faith-formation sessions at the residence or other shared space.

Getting Started

Through the positive recognition of the differences in our individual abilities, you can enhance the unity of the Body of Christ. Here are some introductory suggestions for helping children with special needs.

- **Orthopedic Impairment**—Adapt activities to fit the needs of those with orthopedic impairment; develop a "buddy system"; anticipate and prepare in advance for situations in which a child's symptoms might be disruptive to the group; encourage social interaction; use appropriate terminology when referring to disabilities.

- **Visual Impairment**—Consider range of vision and lighting needs when seating a child; provide large-print, audio, and manual materials; in activities, use other senses besides sight; allow the child to do work orally; assign a partner for visual activities.

- **Deaf or Hearing Impairment**—Seat the child near the front and face him or her when you speak; speak clearly, using a normal tone and pace; write key words and directions on the board; provide written materials; encourage social interaction; work with your catechetical leader and the family to arrange for an interpreter.

- **Speech or Language Impairment**—Speak distinctly and in short phrases; use visual and written instructions as well as oral; work individually in a separate area with the child whose oral work needs attention; allow extra time for the child to respond to your questions and comments.

- **Social/Behavioral Problems, Attention Disorders, Learning Disabilities**—Work with the family to identify the type of disorder/disability; arrange the room to avoid distractions; provide structure and routine; give specific tasks that are interesting to the child; give, review, and clarify clear directions, expectations, and explanations; frequently monitor and affirm appropriate behavior; provide immediate feedback; develop nonverbal clues for unacceptable behavior; break down tasks into smaller, less overwhelming components; use flash cards; introduce skills one at a time; use visual aids and kinesthetic cues (movement, gestures); set up situations in which the child will experience success; frequently assess the child's understanding.

• **Mental Impairment**—Adapt activities to the child's attention span and levels of coordination and skill; individualize learning by using an aid; simplify concepts and repeat periodically; arrange for gifted children to help the slower learners.

Summary: Wonderfully Made

Disabilities are the "normal, anticipated outcomes of the risks, stresses, and strains of the living process."—Mary Jane Owen, NCPD, 2000

"Each of us is willed, each of us is loved, each of us is necessary."—Pope Benedict XVI

I praise you, because I am wonderfully made;
wonderful are your works!
My very self you know.
My bones are not hidden from you,
When I was being made in secret,
fashioned in the depths of the earth.
Your eyes saw me unformed;
in your book all are written down;
my days were shaped, before one came to be. (Ps. 139:14–16, NABRE)

Jesus' command to make disciples does not stop short of persons with special needs. Psalm 139 assures us that in whatever condition we enter this world, God has a divine purpose for each of us. We cannot presume to fathom how God communicates with his children who are without language, who have limited sensory perception, who learn differently, or who have severe physical or mental challenges. In the same way, we cannot fathom the blessings we will miss if these children remain hidden, ignored, or otherwise kept at a distance. By retracing the steps that Jesus took, we won't get lost. Face them in love. Recognize their dignity. Engage with them and invite them to journey together to the eternal destiny of those who love and serve God and one another.

For Reflection and Discussion

- Is there a difference between welcoming and belonging? Consider this question from two vantage points: the subject and the object of welcome. Schedule time for conversations on this topic with people who have disability challenges, both people born with disabilities and those who have acquired them.
- How can you broaden the conversation in your parish about ministering to those with special needs? Who should be "at the table" for those discussions?

Growing as a Catechetical Leader

How would you describe your own level of awareness on this subject? Consider your personal experiences or close encounters with disability. Do you view people with disabilities as having "inestimable value . . . masterpieces of God's creation, made in his own image, destined to live forever," as Pope Francis noted in a message before the Day for Life, 2013? Identify ways people with disabilities can serve the parish, and reach out to them in welcoming friendship.

What provisions are in place in your parish now that serve the needs of the disability community? Identify the gaps to be filled. If change is needed, pray for the courage to make it happen.

Go to www.loyolapress.com/ECL to access the worksheet.

Suggested Action

List the areas of special needs that were mentioned in this chapter. Do you know anyone in your parish/catechetical setting who has one of these special needs? Identify the areas in which you have had direct experience. In what area(s) do you need more knowledge or understanding in order to better adapt your catechetical formation? Build up your skills in order to meet these special needs that exist now or may surface in the future. (The University of Dayton's Virtual Learning Community for Faith Formation [VLCFF] offers a certification track of online courses on disability ministry. To access more resources, visit the Web site for the National Catholic Partnership on Disability at www.ncpd.org.

For Further Consideration

Portions of this chapter were adapted from the adaptive program *Finding God: Our Response to God's Gifts, Catechist Guide* (Chicago: Loyola Press, 2016).

Guidelines for the Celebration of the Sacraments with Persons with Disabilities (Washington, DC: United States Conference of Catholic Bishops, 1978).

National Catholic Partnership on Disability (NCPD). www.ncpd.org.

Pastoral Statement of U.S. Catholic Bishops on Persons with Disabilities (Washington, DC: United States Conference of Catholic Bishops, 1978, 1995).

Welcome and Justice for Persons with Disabilities: A Framework of Access and Inclusion (Washington, DC: United States Conference of Catholic Bishops, 1998).

10

A Unique Community of Faith: Catechesis in the Catholic School

The Totality of the Catholic Faith

Catholic schools have enjoyed a long tradition of high-quality education, firm discipline, and the instilling of Catholic values. Presently, more than sixty-five hundred Catholic schools in the United States are educating nearly two million students. In many jurisdictions, parents can select from a pool of excellent public, charter, and private schools as well. So what distinguishes Catholic schools, and why do they exist?

As stated in the *National Directory for Catechesis*, "Catholic schools . . . exist in order to educate the whole person: mind, body, and soul. They present the totality of the Catholic faith" (*NDC*, #61A.4b). Today, more than ever, the challenge for Catholic schools, and for parish religious-education programs, is to ensure that effective catechesis is taking place.

A Personal Story

As a product of Catholic schools from kindergarten through high school, I had high expectations for my children when we enrolled them in a Catholic school in the 1990s. Our parish school had closed several years before my children were born, so we enrolled them in a neighboring Catholic school. Unfortunately, my expectations were dashed. From all outward appearances, this was a bona fide Catholic school. Inside, the building was adorned with crucifixes, statues, and sacred art; the students wore uniforms. In reality, however, the instruction and practice of the Catholic faith was downplayed because, as they explained, about 80 percent of the student body was not Catholic.

This caused me to pause and reflect on the core identity and purpose of a Catholic school. I knew that children who were enrolled in a Jewish, Muslim, or evangelical Christian school received religious instruction and observed the requirements of that faith. Why, then, would a Catholic school retreat from its mission in order to accommodate students who are not Catholic?

Thankfully, a few years later, our family's experience at another Catholic school was completely different. Community spirit and high academic standards were present. More important, the school's Catholic identity was infused throughout the curriculum and was evident in the staff. The experience in both of these schools has led me to continue reflecting upon the nature, purpose, goal, and identity of Catholic schools. All of these considerations are important for you as a catechetical leader if your role includes responsibility for faith formation in a Catholic school.

The Challenge of Catholic Education

Over the years, I've spoken with catechetical leaders who are asking the same questions I've posed above. Those who have the role of providing faith formation in the Catholic school often find themselves dealing with issues such as the amount of class time dedicated to teaching religion and the extent to which Catholic identity is infused and practiced throughout the curriculum. Likewise, catechetical leaders in poorer parishes often have fewer and poorer-quality resources and materials at their fingertips than their counterparts in wealthier parish schools enjoy.

As a catechetical leader in a Catholic school, you know that "whether a Catholic school is inter-parochial, regional, diocesan, or private, education in the faith is central to its mission" (*NDC*, #61B). In other words, effective catechesis is undoubtedly a defining characteristic of Catholic schools. Once the school's mission is understood, the effectiveness of catechesis in Catholic schools is predicated upon having a well-formed catechetical team and plan. Pope Benedict XVI described the vision succinctly, reaching the heart of the matter: "First and foremost every Catholic educational institution is a place to encounter the living God who in Jesus Christ reveals his transforming love and truth." Students in Catholic educational institutions (regardless of the students' religious affiliation or lack of affiliation) should have many opportunities to encounter the living God. In the daily example of teachers and staff, the lessons of any subject, exchanges with other students, various assignments, and even in reprimands—in all these ways students should find evidence of God's presence.

In *The Case for Catholic Education: Why Parents, Teachers, and Politicians Should Reclaim the Principles of Catholic Pedagogy* (Angelico Press, 2015), Ryan Topping takes a deep dive into three purposes of Catholic education: happiness, culture, and virtue. The author states, "The ends of a Catholic education are the acquisition of heavenly happiness (final goal), formation in a vibrant moral and intellectual culture (proximate goal) and useful skills (immediate goal)" (69). Topping's view overrides pat answers about investing in a good education to get into a good college, land a great job, etc. Instead, he posits that a good Catholic education should put one on the path to one's eternal destiny while shaping the journey and adding an assortment of necessary skills.

Topping is on solid ground when he asserts that the current crisis in Catholic education is not due to academic deficiency. Studies show that Catholic-school graduates succeed professionally and tend to earn more money. We have only to look at the number of Congressional members, justices on the Supreme Court, heads of corporations, and leaders in other fields to recognize the economic benefits of a Catholic education. The real challenge facing Catholic schools, as with all of our catechetical and ministerial efforts, is forming young people into disciples of Jesus Christ.

Enter the Catechetical Leader

In order for this goal to be achieved, many Catholic schools turn to people like you, the parish catechetical leader, to coordinate, animate, and lead the effort. In addition to the many responsibilities you have as a catechetical leader, your role description may also include responsibility for faith formation in the parish Catholic school. Here is a sample of some things you may be asked or expected to do in order to fortify the school's Catholic identity and mission.

- **Selection of Resources**—Together with the principal, the pastor, the religion teachers, and perhaps the school board, you may assist in the selection of resources (such as a textbook series/ curriculum) to be used in faith-formation/religion classes. You may provide in-service training for the religion teachers (often in cooperation with the publisher of the textbook series) to equip them to use the materials most effectively.

- **Implementation of Diocesan Curriculum Guidelines**—Connected with the above, you may coordinate the school's implementing diocesan curriculum guidelines for faith formation.

- **Faculty Faith Formation**—Often, you may coordinate and provide faith-formation experiences for the entire faculty and staff, including retreat days. This helps ensure that the school faculty and staff are themselves being formed in the Catholic faith and empowered to live as disciples of Christ. In some cases, you may need to facilitate the diocesan catechist certification for religion teachers, as well as fulfill the diocesan requirements for all Catholic teachers in the basics of Catholic faith.

- **Liturgical Life**—A significant responsibility for many parish catechetical leaders is the coordination of all school liturgical celebrations, celebrations of the sacraments (such as penance and reconciliation) and observations of the seasons and feasts of the Church's liturgical year. You may also be asked to oversee the formation and training of student liturgical ministers.

- **Prayer Experiences**—Closely tied to assisting in the school's liturgical life is the expertise you can bring in the area of prayer. Many Catholic-school teachers need assistance in developing skills for leading various types of prayer and in preparing and leading prayer services.

- **Service and Social Justice**—A major aspect of Catholic life is participation in acts of mercy, charity, and social justice. You may be asked to coordinate opportunities for young people to serve others through works of mercy and to transform society through social justice. An important part of this is showing students that these actions flow from the gospel message and from Church teaching. You can help them reflect on how they are encountering Christ and growing as disciples through participation in these acts.

- **Peer Ministry**—Many Catholic schools establish programs of peer ministry, in which older students are formed and trained to lead faith-formation experiences (such as retreat days and service experiences) for younger students. They may also serve as liturgical ministers and prayer leaders. You may play a role in coordinating this program and in the formation of peer ministers.

- **Catholic Identity**—One of your responsibilities may be to work with the pastor, principal, faculty, staff, and school board to assess and build up the school's Catholic identity according to diocesan guidelines.

- **Interdisciplinary Efforts**—Some Catholic schools have made great strides in developing interdisciplinary efforts that reinforce Catholic values, teachings, and Tradition across the various subjects in the curriculum. You may be asked to coordinate and bolster such efforts.

- **Parent Meetings and Board Meetings**—It is common for parish catechetical leaders to be involved in the formational and spiritual aspects of various meetings for parents, school board, athletic club, and so on. Responsibilities may range from leading prayer to providing basic spiritual/faith formation for attendees at such meetings.

- **Sacramental Preparation**—Preparing young people for the sacraments is the responsibility of the parish. Thus, you will most likely be responsible for coordinating the sacramental preparation of children in the Catholic school. This includes a children's catechumenate, first holy communion and first reconciliation preparation, and confirmation preparation, as well as providing opportunities for penance and reconciliation and immediate preparation for such opportunities.

- **Curator of Resources**—Finally, as the parish catechetical leader, you are in the unique position of being the Catholic school's curator of Catholic resources—from books, videos, CDs, and online resources to statues, holy cards, rosaries, and scapulars!

While this is not an exhaustive list, the truth is that you may be called upon to do less than what appears above or you may be called upon to do more! The extent of your responsibilities should be negotiated in your hiring and yearly performance appraisal and should be spelled out in your role description.

Wheel inside the Wheel

As in the prophet Ezekiel's "wheel inside the wheel" vision, most Catholic schools are an evangelizing community within the evangelizing community of the parish. Wheels of faith turn other wheels of faith. The movement of the Holy Spirit in the school can enliven the parish, while the parish provides opportunities to practice lessons of faith introduced in the classroom. As such, the parochial school is charged with carrying out a parish vision of formation that is consistent with the diocesan plan and conveys the complete message of faith. Parents, teachers, catechists, catechetical leaders, and pastors should be of one accord on matters of faith formation. Catholic schools are a gift to the Church that can and should be reaffirmed, strengthened, and supported so that they continue to form current and future generations of disciples of Christ.

Summary: Show Them the Way They Are to Live

Teach them his decrees and instructions, and show them the way they are to live and how they are to behave. (Exod. 18:20, NIV)

In remarks given at a Catholic School Symposium in 2015, Denver Archbishop Samuel J. Aquila stated that "the goal of Catholic education is to help parents raise saints." While this may seem like hyperbole at first blush, this is precisely the goal of all catechetical formation, including in Catholic schools. Our mission is to form disciples of Christ. Today, this challenge is more difficult than ever, given the changes that have taken place in our society, not least of which is the changing nature of the family in recent decades. Still, Catholic schools are on the front lines of efforts to help parents raise saints. As a parish catechetical leader, you may play an integral part in your parish school's efforts to carry out this mission.

During the wilderness experience of the Jewish people, Moses sometimes acted as a judge in disputes. One time, Moses's father-in-law, Jethro, observed the crowds pressing in on Moses. Jethro was concerned and asked Moses what the people needed. Moses replied that in addition to settling disputes, the people wanted him to teach them God's statutes. Jethro knew Moses needed relief and support, and he urged him to appoint others to assist him in his efforts to "teach them his decrees and instructions, and show them the way they are to live and how they are to behave."

Today, Catholic schools continue to contribute greatly to the Church's efforts to teach the Lord's decrees and instructions and to show young people and their families how to live as disciples of Christ. As a catechetical leader, you play no small role in creating the next generation of saints.

For Reflection and Discussion

- How is your parish school helping parents to "raise saints"?
- How can you assist your parish school in making these efforts more effective?
- What actions can you take to bring the parish school and parish closer together?

Growing as a Catechetical Leader

As you well know, there can often exist a tension between the Catholic school and the parish religious-education program. As a catechetical leader, you hold the key to bridging that gap. While the school principal is probably not going to be asked to do too much for the parish religious-education program, you may be deeply involved in the work of the school. You can use this to your advantage. Pray about ways to build

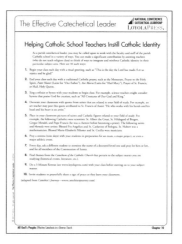

bridges between school children/families and parish religious-education children/families, between teachers and catechists, and, of course, between yourself and the principal.

Go to www.loyolapress.com/ECL to access the worksheet.

Suggested Action

No doubt your diocese has an office for Catholic schools/education that coordinates all the efforts to ensure Catholic schools live up to the criteria that make them uniquely Catholic. Be sure to check out the Web site for your diocesan office in order to familiarize yourself with school policies and curriculum guidelines in the areas of religious instruction/faith formation. Also, explore your parish school's unique identity: its patron saint and/or the charism of the religious order that may have founded it. Avoid coming in with your own preconceived notions; instead, build on the legacy of the school and its stated mission and identity.

For Further Consideration

At the Heart of the Church: Selected Documents of Catholic Education. Ronald Nuzzi, ed. (Notre Dame, IN: Alliance for Catholic Education Press, 2012).

Architects of Catholic Culture: Designing and Building Catholic Culture in Catholic Schools. Timothy J. Cook (Washington, DC: National Catholic Education Association, 2001).

The Case for Catholic Education: Why Parents, Teachers, and Politicians Should Reclaim the Principles of Catholic Pedagogy. Ryan N. S. Topping (Kettering, OH: Angelico Press, 2015).

Catholic Ministry Formation Directory (Washington, DC: Center for Applied Research in the Apostolate, 2015).

United States Conference of Catholic Bishops: Catholic Education, http://www.usccb.org/beliefs-and-teachings/how-we-teach/catholic-education/index.cfm.

The National Catholic Education Association (NCEA, www.ncea.org).

About the Author

Ms. Donna Toliver Grimes resides in Washington, DC. She is the Assistant Director for African American Affairs at the United States Conference of Catholic Bishops (USCCB) in the Secretariat of Cultural Diversity in the Church. Previously, she served USCCB by sharing Catholic social teaching with parish, diocesan, educational groups, and other Catholic organizations. She is a member of the steering team for Christian Churches Together and formerly served as a national advisor for Pax Christi USA.

Ms. Grimes is an experienced catechist, parish catechetical leader, and social justice educator and advocate who has served on a variety of boards and committees at parish, diocesan, and national levels. She graduated from the University of Virginia with an undergraduate degree in Education and is a life-long learner.

Donna Grimes authored a book of Advent reflections for Pax Christi USA, was a regular contributing writer for *Halleluia People* and has written magazine articles for NCCL and *Network Connection*. This mother of three adult children is a Cursillista whose parish is St. Teresa of Avila.

The Effective Catechetical Leader Series

Whether you are starting out as a catechetical leader or have been serving as one for many years, **The Effective Catechetical Leader** series will help you use every aspect of this ministry to proclaim the Gospel and invite people to discipleship.

Called by Name
Preparing Yourself for the Vocation of Catechetical Leader

Catechetical Leadership
What It Should Look Like, How It Should Work, and Whom It Should Serve

Developing Disciples of Christ
Understanding the Critical Relationship between Catechesis and Evangelization

Cultivating Your Catechists
How to Recruit, Encourage, and Retain Successful Catechists

Excellence in Ministry
Best Practices for Successful Catechetical Leadership

All God's People
Effective Catechesis in a Diverse Church

Each book in **The Effective Catechetical Leader** series is available for $13.95, or the entire series is available for $65.00.

To Order:
Call **800.621.1008** or visit **loyolapress.com/ECL**

The ECL App

Everything You Need to Be an Effective Catechetical Leader

The ECL app puts wisdom and practical help at your fingertips. Drawn directly from the six books of **The Effective Catechetical Leader** series, ECL provides an opportunity for catechetical leaders to center themselves spiritually each day, focus on specific pastoral issues, and identify go-to strategies for meeting the challenges of serving as an effective catechetical leader.

Special Features:

- Over 40 unique guided reflections tailored to your individual pastoral ministry needs.
- On-the-go convenience and accessibility on your phone or tablet.
- Modern design, easy-to-use interface, and a source of calm amidst the busy schedule of a catechetical leader.

WELCOME TO ECL

Everything you need to be an effective catechetical leader

ENTER

For more details and to download the app, visit
www.loyolapress.com/ECL